The Wealth Principle

The Wealth Principle

Unleash the Entrepreneur within You

Gregory M. Luchak

RBI ENTERPRISES

A DIVISION OF 1828218 ONTARIO LIMITED

★★★★★

The Wealth Principle™

Paperback Edition

ISBN: 978-1988624075

Disclaimer:

Efforts have been made to verify information contained within this publication. The author and publisher assume no responsibility for errors, omissions, or any inaccuracies. References to the economy and conditions may not reflect the current time period for the reader. We think you will agree that the messages from the information contained in this book are timeless.

Although it is the purpose of this book to educate the reader and all other users based on the information contained in this publication, the author and publisher cannot guarantee that the use of this information will result in any profits to the users.

All readers of this book should be aware that earning profits in real estate, business, or investing can be difficult and challenging. Although many do well with real estate and business ownership, not all make money or a profit. Using this material in conjunction with the appropriate coaching, mentoring, and counseling is advised.

While this book is full of useful practical information, it is not intended to be legal or accounting advice. All readers are instructed to seek competent legal and accounting advice and to follow and apply all laws and regulations that may apply. The reader of this publication assumes all responsibility for the use of the information contained herein. The author and publisher assume no responsibility or liability whatsoever on behalf of the reader of this publication.

The Wealth Principle

Unleash the Entrepreneur within You

Gregory M. Luchak

The color *purple* has a unique meaning throughout the world. Often associated with royalty, nobility, luxury, power, and ambition, the color *purple* also represents wealth, creativity, wisdom, dignity, grandeur, devotion, peace, pride, mystery, independence, and magic. Spiritually, the color *purple* also represents the future, imagination, dreams, and calming of emotions. It inspires and enhances psychic ability and spiritual enlightenment and at the same time keeps us grounded. To us, it simply means *hope*.

Being that our mission for the **Planet Purple** brand is becoming one of *hope*, we plan to give approximately 10 percent of our revenue from every sale of this book to charity. Throughout the years, we plan to support certain events by donating to those charities that meet our guidelines and expectations.

Members of our family and likely yours have been affected by a disease such as blindness, diabetes, or Crohn's or had a sick child, a family member, or another individual who simply needs the help of the community. Visit the Planet Purple website to learn more about our charitable initiatives.

To learn more or to buy a product, scan the QR code.

We hope that part of the reason you buy a product bearing our **Planet Purple** brand is to support people in need not just in our own community but around the world as well.

We believe it is a symbol of hope.

Thank you in advance for your support.

The Planet Purple

www.PlanetOttawa.ca/pages/planet-purple

Dedication

I have always had a passion for business, real estate, and investing. Often having great ideas and concepts that I tried to implement throughout my career, I had to learn the hard way, through trial and error. Obviously, I made many mistakes on my journey. But I persevered. I learned to ask questions and developed an interest in learning how to become an entrepreneur. I keep learning every day.

The knowledge I acquired through trial and error, attending countless seminars, reading many books, and listening to mentors helped me on my journey. I trusted in what I learned. I know that the principles I now write about helped me.

I dedicate this book to all those who have the courage and conviction to pursue their dreams. I also dedicate this book to my children and to my wife, who especially has put up with my endless business endeavors in the pursuit of my dreams.

I encourage you to keep studying, learning, and growing in all areas of your life, and remember, all the information in the world is only as powerful as the amount of action you put behind it.

I look forward to hearing about your story and success one day.

Sincerely,

Greg Luchak

Contents

Testimonials

"I have known Greg for many years and have the highest respect for his business expertise and knowledge. On several occasions, I have used his renovation skills to upgrade my home as well as to prepare my home for sale. Which I sold quickly. I have and would highly recommend Greg to anyone looking for his expertise."

—Frank Kannemann, Ottawa, ON

"I cannot say enough good things about Greg Luchak and his work. We hired Greg and his team to put a large addition on our 1920s home, renovate the second floor, and then hired him back to renovate our kitchen and first-floor bathroom. Greg is honest, steady, straightforward, and thorough and careful in his work. He calmly and competently dealt with all the challenges that arose during the months of working on our house. He was always cheerful. He never lost his cool, never said anything derogatory to us about our old house and its many quirks, and always had his work under control. Greg provided excellent customer service to us. He did us many favours, and always alerted us to potential extra costs. The value of our home was increased by the suggestions and renovations that Greg provided and helped tremendously with the sale of our home. We actually tried to sell our house unrenovated, with no takers, a few years before Greg came along and transformed the house."

—Julie Swettenham, Ottawa, ON

"We had never used a contractor before and were somewhat apprehensive. We were so thrilled with Greg! He is meticulous in his work, his attention to detail is extraordinary, and he has great taste and brilliant suggestions on how to make your room or home look the best. Have referred him to other friends who have been equally impressed. Already planning to have him back again."

—Dean and Amanda Melway, Ottawa, ON

"From knowing Greg for over ten years, *trustworthy* and *friendly* are two words that describe him very well. Whether it's an indoor, outdoor, small or large project, he always applies the same level of thoughtfulness, hard work, and attention to detail to each of them. Unsurprisingly, the results are always above my expectations."

—Greg Brezinia, Kanata, ON

Preface

The purpose of this book originally was to be the first chapter in my training program—My Greatest Business and Investor Training Program. I believed that the content was so important that I decided to make it my first book in print as a prequel to the training program.

Over the past forty years, I had thought about writing a book. My first idea was to try writing a fiction novel when I was in my late teens. I never put a pen to paper, but I had many ideas. My first attempt at writing was a book on a topic that I was very passionate about at the time—real estate investing.

That attempt was called *The Real Estate Evaluation Check List*. It was simple, to the point, and short—only about forty pages long. I registered the title but never took it to print. That was 1988. It was many years later that the idea to write again crept into my psyche. In my forties, I thought I might try to write a movie script. I wrote one page to see if I could do it. (Apparently, one page is equivalent to about sixty seconds of film.) But I never followed through with the whole movie script idea.

It came to me that I had taken many real estate seminars over the years. I learned many things about real estate on my own, but I always craved more knowledge. In 2007, I decided I was going to create a spreadsheet that I could use to analyze my real estate deals. The project kind of morphed from there into a substantial tool. I could effectively enter data and create forecasts. I could predict market values using the same data sets that appraisers use. I could use the data to analyze different strategies to invest in real estate and predict which strategy would be the best.

When I figured this out, it just came to me that I could package this as a product or service to potential clients. My imagination went a little wild. I was inspired. I decided at that point that if I were to do this that the program would need a help page. That idea morphed into a full-blown training on how to use the spreadsheet—hence the creation of Real Business Investors Software. I was using Microsoft Excel and had created a series of macros and formulae.

Having decided to try to make something out of this, I thought I would need to write a complete training manual, which I would call *My Greatest Business and Investor Training Program*. I also realized that over the course of my construction and business career, many of my clients were individuals, developers, or businesses that were in fact renovating or building to flip property. Not only had I invested in several successful real estate deals on my own, but most of my clients had too! I knew I had something of value that I could share with the world.

So I developed and wrote about a dozen chapters that covered topics like how to start a business, wealth protection, marketing, real estate strategies, solving credit issues, creative financing, rehabbing, foreclosures, property management, and understanding contracts, to name a few.

I recognized that over the years I had also tried to develop other business opportunities—not just own and operate a construction company. I also did some business consulting. I had a few clients who wanted to start a magazine business and another who wanted to develop a native, culturally inspired travel book. I helped another friend start up a hair studio. I got involved with a multilevel marketing company. I also developed an online business when the web was just starting to become something big. Transitioning from just text to graphic capability, I carried on that website for almost twenty years. Starting while the Internet was in its infancy, relatively speaking, I operated that website and in the process, became a webmaster. I helped several clients create and manage their websites.

Over the course of my life, I have learned from trial and error, reading, attending seminars, making decisions, making mistakes, and picking myself up again and again. I learned a lot in the process about business and about success.

I have now decided to make it my mission. I have finally defined my purpose and have a clear idea what I can offer people. I have found a new passion. I like to write. I like to help people, and I believe I now have an abundance of experience that I can share.

Developing this book, *The Wealth Principle*, I believe has not only brought some clarity to my business life but will also help others to do the same as they read it. I encourage anyone who can find his or her passion to apply the principles I write about. Clearly, to me, they are essential to success on many levels.

Introduction

*T*he *Wealth Principle* is sprinkled with quotes, statistics, personal stories, and suggestions. You will find that the content and stories I relate to are part of my story. Because of my experience, most of which is in real estate investing and construction, the focus of the book is on entrepreneurship. If you follow the principles and apply them to your story, you can and will find success for yourself as well.

I decided to begin the process, your journey through the book, by talking about economics and how they have impacted our lifestyles today. Where does all our precious money go?

I follow that up with several chapters on the importance of discovering your purpose and how to develop the right attitude and mind-set, as well as how to unleash your entrepreneurial spirit.

To get you off on the right foot in business, I discuss how you can build your empire with a safe business strategy that will allow you to protect your wealth.

Being that I have experience in many areas of business, I talk about how you can pursue different business interests—how to find money and how to use successful strategies to invest in real estate. For those who are credit challenged or simply have no access to capital, I talk about the perfect business for you. I also decided to add a bonus chapter. I wrap the book up with a blast from the past that showcases a few articles I originally wrote and posted on my website over the past decade. These articles reveal the best strategies to be an effective entrepreneur.

The Introduction

Secret Video

www.TheWealthPrinciple.net/introduction.html

In this book…

Discover how to significantly change your lifestyle and increase your wealth. You will learn the secrets of how to break the common mold of "get a good education and a good job." You will learn what the rich know that you need to know to be successful and free. This book covers the following:

- how the wealthy do it
- how the economy affects your lifestyle
- how to unleash your entrepreneurial spirit
- how to find the magic behind your success
- how to pay off and get out of debt quickly
- how to repair your credit
- how to use credit to your advantage
- how and where to find money
- the secrets to safely invest in real estate
- how to safely build your empire from the ground up
- how to start a business with no money
- the secrets to your success

Every chapter includes a secret video you can get access to by scanning the QR code associated. You will get exclusive access to a video that brings a level of interaction with the book and material that will inspire you to learn more about business and becoming an entrepreneur.

Secret Video #1

www.TheWealthPrinciple.net/chapter_one.html

Chapter 1

How Do the Wealthy Do It?

What the mind can conceive and believe,
it will achieve.
—Napoleon Hill

I likely don't know you personally, but I'm willing to bet that what you would really like to have is a residual-based income, the free time and money to do what you want when you want. Have you ever asked yourself, "How do the wealthy do it? What do they know that most of the population either doesn't know or is not willing to do?" Most people have a fear of losing or doing anything they don't understand.

The wealth principle is more than an idea on paper. It's a formula for success—the success principles that the wealthy understand and implement daily.

I believe most people understand the basics of success, but their perspective is reversed. They believe they need to work hard all their lives to achieve financial success. They believe that the highest education possible will bring them financial success, as will climbing that corporate ladder, working sixty to eighty hours a week.

The rich understand that there is less competition being a business owner than being an employee. Ninety-five percent of the population compete against each other for jobs, hoping their higher education will give them an edge. The rich understand that owning a business is simple by comparison. You don't need a degree or a diploma. You don't even need to fill out an application. You only need to decide and never quit.

The fact is the wealthy work hard and earn more because of how they think. The work they do, in their mind, seems effortless because they have a passion for it.

Some people think that the middle class is disappearing, that there will only be two classes—the rich and the poor—that poverty exists in North America. I don't believe poverty exists. As a wealthy entrepreneur I follow states,

> I believe people have poverty thinking.
> —Dexter Yager

The lifestyle we live today is based on the choices we make, the decisions we make. Becoming wealthy as opposed to becoming poor is a choice. We may have been born into the class or lifestyle our parents chose. But it's up to us individually, as adults, whether we become poor, middle class, affluent, rich, or superrich. Becoming wealthy and successful is a decision, not a right of passage given to us at birth.

The wealth principle is about how you think about life, money, and success and how you can create your own destiny. Leaders are readers. Not that you should just continue reading my book—you should read many books on a regular basis. Once you have read this book, you will no longer be able to say that you don't know how to become wealthy and successful. Success isn't just about the money. Success is about the journey. The road you take is a decision. How long you want to travel on that road to success is up to you.

You may have heard about the light at the end of the tunnel and be hoping it isn't an oncoming train. The same pattern for success applies to failure as well. Do nothing, and you will succeed at doing nothing every time. Do something, and you will succeed at something. When you begin to understand failure, you will begin to succeed.

> If you can change your perspective, change the way you think, you can change your life.
> —Gregory M. Luchak

If you can change your perspective, change the way you think, you can change your life. You can put yourself on the track to success just as easily as the track to failure. That oncoming train can either be success or failure, and it is your choice.

So where does all our precious money go? In order to look at this question, we need to understand some basic economic factors and the changes in the economy over the past fifty years. To start, how money, debt, and wealth are created has significantly changed since 1971. The Nixon government was instrumental in finally converting what was once known as the *gold standard*, supporting the US dollar. Since that time, debt and inflation are what support the value of the US dollar. The US dollar is the world currency that all currency is measured against.

In the 1960s, the average home was measured at 200 percent of income. A new single-family home on average cost about $15,000, and incomes in the $7,500 range were normal. Seventy percent of families owned homes and were single-income families. By 1975, it took 300 percent of the average median household income to buy a house. By 2005, it was 470 percent of household income, making it imperative for the middle-class family to include two income earners. According to Canadian Prime Minister Trudeau, the middle class consists of up to four income earners. Today, it takes a whopping 500 to 600 percent of a middle-class-household to afford to buy a house.

In Canada, in the mid-1980s, we experienced a soft market crash, where housing prices stagnated, lessening the blow the financial markets made with double-digit interest rates. In 2009, the United States experienced a hard market crash, where they witnessed housing prices plummet by 50 to 60 percent of their value.

Household incomes since 1995 have significantly stagnated. The only thing that has been allowing this to work are low interest rates and inflation—meaning our governments and banking systems cannot afford real estate markets to crash. The subprime lending market, meaning high-risk loans to low-income earners, are a threat to financial market stability. As I just stated, look at what happened in the United States and Canada in the financial and real estate markets over the past thirty years. In the United States, the housing bubble finally burst, and in certain markets in Canada, like Vancouver and Toronto, everyone is wondering when it will burst there.

On average, statistically, debt rises year over year by 5.1 percent, yet disposable income has only been rising by 3.4 percent. The gap is inflation and a reduction in purchasing power. The only people who are really benefiting by the gap are the affluent, rich, and super rich—the wealthy. Seventy percent of all households today are indebted. Twenty-six percent have a combination of mortgage and consumer debt. Thirty-five percent of households have only consumer debt. To simplify these statistics, the share of household debt is split at 77 percent toward a mortgage and 23 percent toward consumer debt. Measured by percentage of GDP, Canadians are at 100.5 percent, and Americans are at about 78.2 percent of GDP.[1] Consumer debt means store credit and credit cards. Consumer debt is at record highs of 167.6 percent of income in Canada[2]—the highest of the G7 countries. North Americans owe trillions of dollars in student loans, credit card debt, auto loans, and mortgages. Low-income and middle-class earners are borrowing against their equity to pay for their lifestyle. Statistics also show that low-income earners carry the highest percentage of debt, while the wealthy carry the lowest.

---

[1] *Canada Households Debt to GDP*, (Trading Economics. 2017) https://tradingeconomics.com/canada/households-debt-to-gdp#Household_Debt_To_GDP_By_Country
[2] *Canadian key household debt ratio hits record high,* (CBC News September 15, 2016) www.cbc.ca/news/business/debt-income-ratio-record-1.3763343.

Canadian and American Median Income Levels

Class	Income	%	Description
The poor	0 to $54,000	20	low-income earners, two income earners
The middle class	$54,000 to $108,000	75	employed, self-employed typically, two to four income earners per household
The affluent	$100,000 to $1,000,000	3	employed, self-employed, small business owners
The rich	$1,000,000 per year	> 1	independent business owners
The superrich	$1,000,000 per month		and investors

My point here is that the wealthy perceive the use of debt differently than the average person. Income-wise, you want to be affluent at a minimum, as shown in the table above. If your goals are higher and you want to be independently wealthy, you need to be in the 1 percent club. The danger zone is where the masses are, where 95 percent of North Americans reside.

Experts state that the Great Recession of the new millennium was from 2007 to 2009.[3] There were brief examples of a recovery from 2010 to 2012. I believe it started earlier in 2006, and for many people, it hasn't really ended yet. In 2012, they believe the market reset to 360 percent of income to buy a home in the United States. By banking standards, that puts our financial stability in a critically high-risk position. Debt servicing cannot exceed 35 percent of income, based on the PITH method, to safely pay for debt. All you need to do is some

---

[3]*Great Recession*, (Wikipedia, December 04,2016) https://ipfs.io/ipfs/QmXoypizjW3WknFiJnKLwHCnL72vedxjQkDDP1mXWo6uco/wiki/Great_Recession.html

simple math to figure out where you fit in. The impact on the average person's ability to save money, let alone live on what is being called a living wage is challenging. What is really becoming increasingly scary is that our governments now consider the middle class to be a family of four income earners earning a total of between $54,000 and $108,000 annually,[4] the average being $90,000. If they want to buy a home, they will be spending 600 percent of their combined income, making it exceedingly difficult to own a home. For the first time in almost a century, the next generation will likely be living at a lower standard of living than the previous three generations.

> The distribution of wealth has very little to do with
> what you know or who you know, but more to do with *how you think*!
> —Gregory M. Luchak

Employees, including the self-employed (doctors, lawyers, professionals, tradespeople, bakers, plumbers, small business owners, and so on) make up 95 percent of the population. The affluent, independent business owners and investors make up the other approximately 5 percent. Ironically, independent business owners and investors, "the wealthy," control 90 percent of the wealth, leaving the rest for the majority, mostly employees, to fight over. In fact, 50 percent of the world's wealth is controlled by eight people! You guessed it. They are not employees!

Only the employed rely on what they know and who they know so they can get hired. It's no wonder that the poor and middle class struggle to make it. All the control is with the affluent, the rich, and the superrich. Statistically, only 3 percent of people will be affluent and less than 1 percent will be rich. Isn't it also ironic that the wealthy on average only have a high school education or less? Eighty percent, in fact. At the least, that is what I have been told. It's also a fact that only 20 percent inherit wealth. The rest are self-made. So, what do they, the rich, do that makes them so wealthy? To start with, they employ the

---

[4]Robin, Raizel. *Canada's Middle Class Is on the Brink of Ruin.* (The Walrus, May 17, 2017)
https://thewalrus.ca/canadas-middle-class-is-on-the-brink-of-ruin/.

educated, the middle class, and the poor. They understand that the key to financial success is leverage and duplication.

Your future is created by what you do today, not by what you will do tomorrow! Your financial success is measured by what you did yesterday and the day before. More jobs have been lost in the past forty years than have been created. The 95 percent are delusional about their job security. They spend more money than they earn and reward themselves even if they can't afford it. The proof of this is the amount of consumer debt North Americans are currently sitting on. Eighty percent will become dependent on others to help them, and one-third will have no savings when they retire.

According to recent studies,[5] there is a massive gap in necessary retirement savings. On average, North Americans are short by at least $500,000. What does that mean? Most Canadians have no savings and no financial plan that will cover the deficit they will need to live into their nineties. The story is much the same in the United States. One out of every three people have nothing saved for retirement. Those who have are short by at least 50 percent. The average American is said to need $360,000 saved by age sixty. Those who have saved have less than $100,000.

To sum up, the difference between the wealthy and the rest of the world isn't a university degree or a good job. They understand that there is more risk being employed than owning a business. The masses, the 95 percenters, believe the reverse. The wealthy have also learned to never quit, to persevere. If you want more money in your life, then you need to be where the money is—in a business and investing your profits.

---

[5]*The Retirement Savings Crisis*. (National Institute on Retirement Security 2017) www.nirsonline.org/index.php?option=content&task=view&id=768.

[5] Frankel, Mathew, *10 stats that prove Baby Boomers are in retirement trouble.* The Motley Fool (USA Today March 3, 2017) https://www.usatoday.com/story/money/personalfinance/retirement/2017/03/0 3/10-statistics-that-prove-baby-boomers-are-in-big-trouble/98526764/

I ask this question: Why doesn't the pension system work? We are taught since birth to get a good education and a good job with what? A pension? Buy a house and pay it off so we can retire happily with no debt. The government believes that we need a three-part retirement plan. First, work hard for forty-five years and qualify for a pension at age sixty-five. Second, get a job with a pension. Third, save money for your retirement. It sounds good in theory, but in practice, that system is broken.

If you go back in time to the Builders Generation (1924–1946), they worked hard and saved money. There were no government pensions, and the average life span for most people was sixty-five to seventy-five years old. The Boomer Generation (1946–1964), the largest sector of the population at the time, are now retiring. They came of age creating the pension system in the 1960s. On average, the boomers had only three jobs. Over half have pension plans and own homes. Most only paid 250 percent of their income to buy that home, but even stating that, major banks have determined that the boomers have already figured out that they will need to sell their homes or go back to work, considering that most will be living into their nineties. Then came Generation X (1964–1980).

Forty percent of our youth are unemployed!

We have condemned our young people to have no place in society…to beg for jobs that no longer exist or fail to promise them a future.
—Pope Francis

Unfortunately, there are not enough of them to pay into the government pension system for it to cover the cost of people retiring today. To compound that, they are averaging between five and ten jobs in their lifetime. Following that, is Generation Y (1980–2000), which many also identify as the Millennial Generation (2000–present). They are now the largest generation in the population and will have more than fifteen jobs in their lifetime.

Today, over 30 percent of the people between the age of fifteen and sixty-four are unemployed.[6] Depending on how you read the statistics. An even higher rate applies to the millennials. They can only find part-time jobs. It has become the Uber economy generation. And it isn't because they're all in school. Half of that demographic cannot afford to get a postsecondary education. Those who can get the education spend the following ten years paying off the debt. The millennials are becoming the most indebted, low-income earners in generations. Government findings show that the middle class is not growing in the labor market.[7]

Compound all that information with the fact that since the 1980s very few people save money anymore. Credit is cheap and available. People are more likely to borrow the money for travel, cars, furniture, food, and housing to complement their lifestyles than save the money and pay cash. Statistics are showing that the average North American has less than $500 in the bank, no savings, and little or no pension plan. The fact is they go through too many jobs to ever qualify to have a pension worth anything substantial. The millennial generation will not have the opportunity for a pension their predecessors did. Part-time jobs just don't cut it.

The US and Canadian pension plans are in trouble, and our governments know it. The cost of home ownership is out of reach for over half of the population. If you go further and examine RRSP or 401(k) investing, you will see most are invested into mutual funds, a retail stock investment program. If you analyze how profits are made in stocks, you will find out that the reason most plans generate less than a 3 percent return is because the money invested is at the highest point

---

[6] Catalyst, *Generations in the Workplace*. (New York: Catalyst, July 20, 2017) www.catalyst.org/knowledge/generations-demographic-trends-population-and-workforce

[7]*Canadian Income Inequality.* (The Conference Board of Canada, 2017) www.conferenceboard.ca/hcp/hot-topics/caninequality.aspx.
America's Shrinking Middle Class. (Pew Research Center, May 11, 2016) www.pewsocialtrends.org/2016/05/11/americas-shrinking-middle-class-a-close-look-at-changes-within-metropolitan-areas/

of sale, not the lowest. The plan holder has no control of when to buy or when to sell. The wholesale price of the stock is typically the price when the company was created and at the initial offering. Mutual funds miss the boat. This isn't a point to create an argument that money cannot be made in the stock market. If you follow Warren Buffet's idea of creating wealth, you need to own stock in companies that are undervalued, have a controlling share of their market, and hold them over a long period—multiple years, in fact—to allow compound interest to work its magic. Unfortunately, most of us don't make the time or have the discipline to study and understand which companies to invest in.

The challenge is that most people don't know how to invest, and their efforts are compounded by the long history of market crashes. Analyzing the economic conditions, you can see pension plans are not affordable for the governments, and the private sector doesn't want the added expense. This is evidenced by the fact that part-time jobs are taking over full-time jobs.[8] Part-time jobs typically do not come with a pension plan. Take into account the average pension is based on 60 percent of the best five years, usually the last five years of full-time employment. If you take the average single income today of $38,000 and the average family income of $65,000, based on 2013, that's approximately $50,000 a year. Sixty percent of that is $30,000 (of taxable income), and that typically includes the government's old-age security pension, as almost all plans top up their plan with those pensions. You couldn't own a home or travel or do any of the things most people will want to do on that kind of income, even if it is indexed to inflation. Keep in mind that only about half of the population will have a nongovernment pension. The rest will only have a government old-age security pension, which is about $1,000 a month. You can't have a lifestyle of your choosing on that little bit of income.

---

[8] *Canada created lots of jobs last year. Almost all were part-time.* (Global News, January 5, 2017) globalnews.ca/news/3163885/canadian-job-growth. Gillespie, Patrick. *America's part-time workforce is huge.* (CNN Money, April 25, 2016) money.cnn.com/2016/04/25/news/economy/part-time-jobs/

If that is your income and you own a home, it better be paid for and you better have no other debt. Do the math.

The pension system is broken. It doesn't work anymore. Not that it ever would have worked in the first place. In my opinion, the only solution to the pension dilemma is to own a business and develop a residual-based income that only increases in value. If you do have a pension, that's great. Something is better than nothing. But if you want options, build a business. Invest in real estate. Become an entrepreneur. Start part time. Do, it in your spare time! Create multiple streams of income.

Are you willing to risk the rest of your life as an employee, fighting for that pension? It doesn't matter how old you are, near retirement age or just starting out. You can quickly build a residual-based business income you can retire on in a short time. It all depends on how hard you are willing to work for it.

Success is a decision—your Decision!
—Gregory M. Luchak

Do you want to be in the same position as the population majority—one paycheck from financial disaster? Then it may be time for you to rethink your position and take a decision.

All the information in the world is only as good as the action you put behind it. The speed of your success is truly dependent on how much action you are willing to take to reach your goals. The world as we know it is changing. Retirement is becoming obsolete. I can think of a better way. Retirement is about lifestyle. Why not build an income around a lifestyle—not based on physical retirement? Do more not less. Learn to work smart and live longer.

The strategy to survive today is to understand the true state of our economy and when and where to invest your time and money. According to Harry S. Dent Jr., an independent economist who wrote the book *The Great Boom Ahead* and has appeared on CNN and in *Businessweek* and is a Harvard Business School graduate.

> This decade has and will be the worst that anyone has seen before.
> —Harry S. Dent Jr.

The years 2008 to 2011, Dent predicted, was the "great crash ahead" during that period. The "great boom ahead" will follow, starting around 2020 to 2023. The last boom was from 1987 until 2007.

We are experiencing the greatest debt bubble in history. This will likely be the most challenging decade of our lifetimes. If you want to succeed, you need to learn how to increase your income and protect your assets. To do this, you need to understand that people are what drive the economy.

Harry Dent Jr. also talks about how, on average, most people enter the workforce at age twenty. By twenty-eight, they start having kids. They buy their first house at age thirty-one, start spending on daycare by age thirty-three. Between the ages of thirty-seven and forty-two, they buy their biggest house. At age forty-six, they spend the most money on their kids' college educations. By the age of fifty, they start looking for a change in lifestyle.

> You can no longer plan to retire at sixty-five and goof off for the next thirty years at the expense of a generation that can't afford it.
> —Harry S. Dent Jr.

They travel the most at age fifty-four. They spend the most on life insurance and financial planning services at age fifty-eight. At age sixty-eight, most spend money on health insurance, and by seventy-eight, it is on pharmaceuticals.[9]

---

[9] Dent, Harry S. Jr., *Your Boom Ahead*, Audio Recording (Accelerate Publishing, 2015).

This data research, as Harry S. Dent Jr. describes, presents itself on average every forty-six years and is predictable.[10] Examine that information across generations, and you can see where we are right now.

In times like this, it is no wonder that people are feeling insecure. Unemployment is not accurately reported by the government. In North America, the average is more like 20 percent, and in many other countries, it exceeds 25 percent. Health care is underfunded. Retirement plans are underperforming, and private debt is in the trillions of dollars.

Are you struggling? Can you see that this is a time of opportunity? You need to start thinking and acting like an entrepreneur. To succeed during this turbulent economic time and be positioned to ride the next boom, you need to develop multiple streams of income. Build a business. Believe in yourself. Believe in people. Believe in what you are doing. Plan for the next ten years. If you want to be a part of the next boom coming soon, by 2023, you need to start now.

---

[10] Dent, Harry S. Jr., *Your Boom Ahead*, Audio Recording (Accelerate Publishing, 2015).

Secret Video #2

www.TheWealthPrinciple.net/chapter_two.html

Chapter 2

Discovering Your Entrepreneurial Spirit

Ninety percent of your success relies
on your character, not your skills.
—Unknown

What is the true definition of an *entrepreneur*?

Becoming an entrepreneur is all the rage today. Millennials literally have little choice but to become entrepreneurs if they are to break the mold as I describe it.

Specifically, entrepreneurs start businesses and by that definition become leaders. The millennial generation has the worst job prospects of any in our recent history. Becoming an entrepreneur is the solution they are looking for.

Gen X become entrepreneurs because they finally realized that they hated their jobs and wanted a change in life, a better lifestyle. Baby boomers often decide to become entrepreneurs out of necessity because they also finally realize that for the past thirty to forty years, they have been working for nothing. The house isn't paid for. They are in debt up to their eyeballs, or they are simply bored of the prospect of retirement. Who wants to retire when you still have a lifetime to live into your nineties or even to one hundred years old?

An entrepreneur is responsible for taking a group of people, creating a team, and putting them to work providing a solution the consumer is looking for. Considering the role of an entrepreneur, it is no wonder that the millennial generation is the most entrepreneurial of our time.

Being an entrepreneur is not a job. Entrepreneurship is a lifestyle choice. Don't be fooled by those who want to claim owning a business is like owning a job. Becoming a business owner is a choice. Like I said earlier, the entrepreneur faces no competition to start a business. It is a simple decision compared to the decision to go to school for academic credentials and then compete in the marketplace for a full-time job that doesn't exist for the majority. And, oh, by the way, only employees have jobs.

Entrepreneurs aren't looking for pensions, weekly paychecks, or handouts. They strive to build value in an idea that can change lives and create wealth for many, not just themselves.

I'd also mention it is important not to confuse what an entrepreneur does with the role of a pioneer. A *pioneer* can start a business and create a team of leaders. But pioneers look to create the need that the consumer eventually will adopt. An entrepreneur is the leader who builds the team and then fulfils a need the consumer already has by providing a better solution than the one that already exists.

You can be both, but as a solution to your need to create wealth, to start, the role of an entrepreneur is what you are looking for. It's faster, more practical, verifiable, sustainable, and realistic. The decision to be an entrepreneur will put you on the side of the economy that will give you the greatest benefit and greatest rewards financially. There are no limitations.

Some say the equation that demonstrates the role of an entrepreneur is as follows:

Entrepreneur = Money + Product x Customers = Business

It's theoretically correct, but I look at the equation and see this:

Entrepreneur / Leadership + Solution x Customers = Success

The money factor, although important, is only a part of the solution. The most important factors are leadership and people. The people are either part of the team, or they are the customer.

Entrepreneurs realize that if they multiply their customers, then they can exponentially multiply the results. Results equal success.

And here is an important thing to understand. I learned this by attending a training seminar when, once upon a time, I worked for Canada Post. The theme to the training was this: everyone you encounter is your customer. If you are the entrepreneur, then your investors, leaders, managers, employees, and all your potential consumers are your customers. You should treat everyone as a customer. Value first. Customer first. The idea of giving value is to be a servant to the masses. The best entrepreneurs are the best servants. As an entrepreneur, you must treat everyone with equal respect. They don't serve you. You serve them with leadership, ideas, and solutions. They in turn serve you by following your ideas and bringing them to the masses. It's a win-win solution to success.

Another trait of an effective and successful entrepreneur is to develop multiple streams of income. Considering most entrepreneurs, just like normal people, have short attention spans, relatively speaking, the reason you want to develop teams of people is so you can have multiple ideas and solutions at work. Own more than one business.

By creating multiple cash-flow scenarios, you can spread the financial risk. Cash flow is the number-one reason next to a lack of marketing that causes business failure. An effective entrepreneur will build a business system that multiplies the cash flow, so business can continue. That means provide more than just one product or service. The rule of thumb is three. Also, own more than one business. Start with one, and then build on that with a second and a third. In the process, you can build wealth.

Have you ever heard of the eighty/twenty rule? This rule can be applied to a lot of areas in life and business. Out of one hundred people, you will find that eighty will have little or no interest. Twenty will have some interest. In sales, 20 percent of your customers will provide eighty percent of your revenue. On another note, 80 percent will likely waste your time.

Learn to *focus*. Not just on the tasks at hand but on where your greatest
advantage for success will be.
—Gregory M. Luchak

Again, 20 percent will pose problems where 80 percent will not.
It seems to be a universal rule.

Warren Buffet and Bill Gates both agreed that the single most
important trait that enabled their success was focus. You need to learn
how to focus not just on the tasks at hand but on where your greatest
advantage for success will be. Look for the 20 percent who will provide
that advantage. As a leader, you are looking for other potential leaders.
You will find them in the top 5 percent—where you are now or where
you are planning to be.

Businesses have seasons, and so should entrepreneurs. Your
business interests should reflect those seasons, so you have continuity.
It sounds a little deep, but it's true.

The idea of the four seasons and business is that in the spring
season of your business, you are sowing the seeds. In the summer
season, you are nurturing your crop. You then harvest in the fall
season. The winter season is when you are rewarded. You then reinvest
and start the process over again. It is also good to recognize that the
business you start may not follow the calendar. Your spring season may
start in the fall season. Understanding your business market is essential
to understanding the four seasons of your business.

The entrepreneur must have or develop the characteristic of
being the leader. I can simplify this for you. I know that many people
think they don't have what it takes to be an entrepreneur. Some think
you must have that alpha trait that causes people to dominate and
overwhelm people. Some perceive the alpha (male) as a bully or a go-
getter. He takes what he wants and hurts people in the process with no
regard. This is not accurate.

Never let anyone steal your dream.
—Dexter Yager

The solution you are looking for is passion. Passion and motivation are not events that happen during your lifetime. They are a lifestyle choice. They can be created, self-observed, and even controlled. You can literally figure out how to motivate yourself and be passionate by observing your own personal thoughts and feelings. Feelings control our thoughts. We recycle our thoughts on a continuous basis. The only competition you have that surrounds you is your own mind. You can learn to live a lifestyle of passion. Understand that passion can create success, and therefore success becomes a decision that you can make—and even predict. The best entrepreneurs have passion, a purpose to fulfil, and a dream they are pursuing. The pursuit of a dream is the ultimate entrepreneurial experience, and everyone should have one.

The pursuit of a dream is really what makes this world what it is. Everything we want, need, or have was created by someone with a dream—what we wear, the food we eat, the homes we live in, the furniture we sit on, the cars we drive, the vacations we take, and everything else you can think of. Someone had a dream and a purpose to fulfil it.

Whatever success you want in life, the driving force for you to succeed will be your dream. Define your dream, create a plan, and then act. Follow through, and never quit. Find your passion, focus, and live with a purpose. Pursue your dreams until you achieve them.

Napoleon Hill spent his lifetime interviewing the most successful people in America and writing about what he discovered. One of his greatest works was the *Law of Success*. Most people are familiar with his most famous book, *Think and Grow Rich*.

Dale Carnegie approached Napoleon Hill at a time when he was just a broke reporter. If you have read enough books and attended enough seminars, you will already know of this pioneer's story. I call him a pioneer, just as many others do, because he was one of the first authors who ended up blazing a trail in the self-improvement industry. He spent a great deal of time interviewing the wealthy—a million-dollar net worth then would be the equivalent of a billion-dollar net worth today.

Now that may not be mathematically correct, but it certainly demonstrates just the kind of people Napoleon Hill interviewed, people who were recognized as the most successful and wealthiest people of their time. Through his investigation and research, he discovered some very significant traits. Rather than repeat what he wrote, I will simply state this: although he exclusively wrote about success principles and broke them down into several books, his book *Law of Success* is the bible of success principles.

I can summarize it for you in this way. In the pursuit of your dream to find your passion, to find your purpose, strive to incorporate the following sixteen laws of success that Napoleon Hill discovered:

1. Discover the power of "the master mind."
2. Have a definite chief aim.
3. Be self-confident.
4. Create a habit of saving.
5. Take the initiative and be a leader.
6. Use imagination.
7. Have plenty of enthusiasm.
8. Act with self-control.
9. Create the habit of doing more than you are paid for.
10. Have a pleasing personality.
11. Use accurate thought.
12. Develop the ability to concentrate.
13. Instill cooperation with others.
14. Learn from failure.
15. Have tolerance for others.
16. Finally, live by the golden rule.

It's not about having a dream. It's about reaching it.
—John Maxwell

As you are discovering, your dreams are the fuel to your success. Your attitude and belief are vitally important attributes to your success. The bigger your dreams become, the bigger your success will be. Learn to think big, dream big, and live big. You will learn that you can't do everything yourself. The more you do yourself, the harder you will work. Self-employed entrepreneurs tend to be control freaks and want to do everything themselves. If you ever want to become an independent business owner, you need to duplicate your efforts. Successful businesses have a system. Your business needs to have a system that you can duplicate and easily manage and that can operate on its own.

The greatest success comes when you can be of service to others—solving a problem, creating a job for someone, helping someone else achieve, putting someone else's needs first.

You need to learn that those who understand the principle of becoming a servant have the innate ability to create success without having to ask or pray to God. Many people pray every day for their circumstances to change but do nothing to be rewarded. Being a servant means bringing something of value to others.

Creating value, whether you believe in divine intervention or not, works. Do it honestly, from the heart. Believing what you do is helping someone not only can be gratifying from a spiritual point of view but may even bring you financial gratification. Sometimes it is delayed gratification, and it may happen when you least expect it. But it is always a reward for something you did in the past not something you promise to do in the future.

Your success will be greatly improved when you counsel with a mentor, someone who can coach you, who can help you stretch out of your comfort zone. It should also be someone who has achieved success and continues to achieve because he or she is still in the game.

You need to follow a leader who is going in the same direction you want to go, someone who can help you with the challenges you will face.

All the information in the world is only as good as the action you put behind it. Your success is truly dependent on how much action you take to reach your goals. Acting means making decisions. Sometimes those decisions are hard to make. You don't know if you're going to fail or succeed. One thing is for sure. You will never find out unless you make the decision to act.

> The path to success is to take massive, determined action.
> —Tony Robbins

Success really is only achieved quickly by taking massive action. You can't do things in a small way. You must be all in. Live off your fear. Don't run from it. Taking that step forward is the only way to stretch, change, and grow. The only way to accomplish a goal is to act on it in a big way. That means do it and never quit or look back.

It's a new year and a new beginning! Have you ever asked yourself this question before: If I keep doing the same thing day in and day out, can I really expect a different result?

The new year, for most people, usually brings new resolutions, new goals, and new dreams. Typically, we all think about quitting some activity or engaging in an activity, for example to lose weight or eat healthier. Maybe you want to make more money, pay off the credit card, or go on vacation. How about spending more time with the family? (Or maybe less time!)

Here is something you may have not heard before. The words we speak have energy! If you really want something bad enough, I suggest you try doing something you might find a little uncomfortable, maybe even radical at first. I guarantee that if you persist with these next four strategies that you will find remarkable results. Here is something to think about: Your passion can eliminate your fear.

People with purpose have a bright outlook on life.
—Kim Kiyosaki

First, you must start by creating new habits and stop the old bad habits. To create a new habit, you must make a conscious effort to repeat the new habit every day. Some of the experts I have listened to say you must repeat the habit a minimum of twenty-one days. I believe that you must repeat that new habit for at least ninety days. It is easy to start something new, but it is difficult to break an old habit, which is why a lot of people revert to their bad habits.

I believe that you should write down your goals daily, every day. You need to imprint that goal, that new habit. You're trying to create a new habit or reach a goal that needs to be drilled into your conscious mind until it becomes normal for your subconscious mind to adopt it into your psyche.

Take out a small notepad with at least one hundred pages. Every day, write down that list of new habits and goals you want to change or adopt. Repeat the list every day for at least ninety days. You can't just write it down once and hope that was enough. I tried that for years. I would write down my New Year's resolutions and then just put the list away to review the following year. Half the time, I didn't even review the list. I was going through some old papers not long ago, and I came across a list I had made thirty years ago, I will tell you that to no surprise to me, I had not achieved most of the things I listed. Why? Because I didn't spend any time imprinting that list of goals. It was literally a hope and a prayer, things I wished for with no action to intervene in the process.

You are never too old to set another goal or to dream a new dream.
—C. S. Lewis

Write down your dreams, complete with a date to reach them. You may never hit the date. But with repetition, you will eventually achieve the goal—because you never want to quit and because you can always reset the date.

If your goal is to lose weight, then one of the best ways I found was to find a simple healthy diet, exercise ten minutes a day, and participate in a group environment. I lost over forty pounds in three months. That's right, ninety days. I created a new habit of eating properly. And although I did gain back about fifteen of those pounds, I have been able to maintain my weight at that level ever since. Being in a group environment kept me accountable to my plan. Be accountable to someone about your new habit.

If you want to be successful with your personal finances, find a mentor. Maybe your dream is to pay off debt, buy a new car with cash, buy a new house, or go on a trip.

Whatever that goal is, the third part of the imprinting equation is to learn to speak what you want into existence.

You may be asking, "How do I do that?" It's simple. Start telling yourself out loud what it is you want. Read your list out loud daily.

Then follow that up by posting pictures of what you want on your cell phone, on your computer, on the fridge, on your mirror. Post them anywhere you can see what you want daily.

Fourth, go out and touch that dream weekly. Maybe it's a car. Go to a dealership and sit in it. Take it for a test drive. Maybe it's a new home. Drive by the one you would like to have as often as you can. Walk through an open house. Do whatever it takes to touch, taste, feel, and smell whatever it is you want in life.

You see, we are emotional creatures, and we think, act, and make decisions emotionally. Once you have made an emotional decision to get that dream, reach that goal, break that bad habit, or start a new good habit, your subconscious will find a way to get it—even if you have no idea in the moment how to do it. Your subconscious mind will steer you in the direction of your conscious decisions—whether you realize it right now or not. Your future is unlimited once you understand the power of a dream or a goal and how to create the habits you need to go out and chase it.

I wanted to include an article I wrote back in 2011 that I posted on my website at that time. It was inspired by a mentor and friend of mine, Andy Argyris, after I listened to an audio recording of a speech he gave. I believe that it is still relevant today and found no better place to include it than right here.

***

Thursday, May 12, 2011

Can a Bald Guy Really Be a Hairdresser?[11]

By Greg Luchak

Master Renovator, Contractor, and Entrepreneur

Have you ever heard of Robert Kiyosaki (*Rich Dad, Poor Dad*)? I'm sure you have. He wrote a book called *Cash Flow Quadrant*, where he described how money, income, and wealth are generated.

According to Robert, basically, there are four areas, or quadrants, where you can earn money.

On the left side of this equation are two quadrants that represent about 95 percent of the general workforce—employees and self-employed.

If you were like me, you likely were or currently are in one of these two quadrants.

Five or six days a week, you would get up at the crack of dawn to get in a car, a bus, or a train and head to work.

You would spend ten to twelve hours a day traveling to work, working at a job you hate, but it pays for something, then traveling back home to get up the next day and repeat the process known as the Rat Race!

---

[11] Articles have been edited for clarity and formatting.

Sound all too familiar?

Employees and self-employed trade their time for dollars. It's called actively participating to earn an income. If they don't show up to work, they don't get paid. They work forty to fifty years and then "retire" on 60 percent of their annual income. Robert Kiyosaki also noted these 95 percent of the workforce only control about 10 percent of the wealth in this world.

For many, that means retiring into poverty.

That's scary!

Robert Kiyosaki also stated that, on the right side of the quadrant are "independent business owners" and "investors." This quadrant represents about 5 percent of the workforce, but they earn "passive income." In other words, they make money without having to be actively involved to do it. Here is an example:

If you owned a MacDonald's franchise, as the owner, you would have invested anywhere from $800,000 to as much as $2 million to own the rights to a franchise and would expect to earn about a 20 percent profit. You don't have to be there to flip burgers or manage, but you get paid anyway.

MacDonald's is touted as the number-one food franchise in the world. I'm sure you could agree with that. But how many people can afford to own one?

The paradox is that business owners and investors, as Robert Kiyosaki states, control 90 percent of the wealth in the world!

So, does it make sense that if you or I want to be financially independent and have the ability to earn more income, that we should actively pursue the ability to be "independent business owners"?

But the concern you might have is *risk*. Agreed!

You don't have $2 million, I'm assuming! In fact, you're likely in debt up to your eyeballs already living paycheck to paycheck! Right? Well, maybe not.

But the fact is that 99 percent of the population spend 110 percent of their disposable income. That's right; I said 110 percent. Wow!

Statistics reveal that on average "household savings" at retirement are less than 5 percent. In fact, most savings accounts are sitting at minus 5 percent, the lowest it has been since 1933—another *wow*!

What if I told you that you could participate in the *right side of the cash flow quadrant risk free*?

Are you ambitious enough to try? Are you coachable?

I will go out on a limb here and say that, ultimately, we all do things we don't really want to do, right?

In fact, you might be thinking that you're not going to do anything that involves selling, talking to strangers, showing my family, and—let's face it—extra time and that four-letter word *work*.

The fact is that starting any kind of business requires all of the above. Whether we like it or not, it involves getting out of our comfort zone, doing things we would not normally do!

The fact is we have all been doing the same things for years, creating habits that keep us broke. Can you learn to do something you think you can't do?

As my good friend, Andy, asks, "Can a bald guy be a hairdresser?"

I'd like to add…

Can a vegetarian own a meat shop?

Can a lady sell men's shoes?

Can a Jamaican be a bobsledder?

The answer is yes, and all these people exist. And all have found success!

So, can you do something you might hate doing in the beginning?

How important is your personal success?

How much is it costing you not to have this information?

You have nothing to lose and everything to gain by getting the right information! The stuff I am talking about is just the tip of the iceberg on what you can learn to be successful.

A decision is the only thing standing between you and your success. This is the first day of the rest of your life, and how you spend it is a choice.

Can you imagine that when I wrote this article, most people were spending 110 percent of their income! Now it's 167 percent! And it's only six years later. Big, big *wow*!

I edited out a few call-to-action lines that took people to another page on my website. But I strongly feel that the message in that letter is as powerful today as it was then.

To unleash your entrepreneurial spirit, you need to decide. Then act. It would be even better for you if you found a mentor, someone you can model yourself after, model your business after. If you spend all your time trying to be a pioneer and reinventing the wheel, that could be extremely hard to do, not to mention the cost of making mistakes. I'm not saying you can't. I'm just saying if you want success relatively quickly, compared to working a job for forty years, it's better to follow and model successful people.

Another pattern for success as an entrepreneur is to build a team of people around you. The biggest success financially comes from the business and business connections that surround your business idea. Whether it be a product or service, the business model I found that will create the greatest success is what I call "the business around the business." It starts with creating a team. That team doesn't have to be employees or hired contractors. It's about personal connections. Whom do you know? Whom are you willing to meet? Whom can you include in your circle of influence?

Most successful entrepreneurs have learned that leverage is the art of duplication. This principle relates to more than the growth of your business. The more "ears" you have on the ground, the more chances you have at finding opportunity. The more opportunities you have, the greater your chance at finding success.

What is a bird dog? What is the bird dog effect?

If you want to go fast, go alone. If you want to go far, go together.
—Holly Branson

Everyone you meet has the potential to pass an opportunity every single day. We all do. But not everyone has the time or money to participate. You would hope that if someone recognizes the opportunity that they would share that knowledge. You should create the habit of finding people who can be that bird dog. If you have more ears to the ground, then the chance of opportunity coming your way will be greater.

Entrepreneurs often pay people to give them information critical to the success of their business, like whether a prime piece of real estate might be available for investment. Sometimes the opportunity to land a contract or hiring the right person for the job at hand came because of someone's word of mouth.

The best information is always talked about before it ever hits the news, the media, or for that matter the public. To be an effective entrepreneur, you should have as many bird dogs as you can. Always leave people with the added benefit that they can also have a piece of the action if they bring you the knowledge you're looking for first.

You can have all the education in the world and even enough money to participate in a great business idea. But if your timing is off, you can, and many do, lose it all.

You buy that stock because it sounds like a great investment. You think the market is going up when it's about to come crashing down. You thought the property you bought was going to double in value, but it didn't. You were the first to market with the next greatest widget, thinking you would control the market, only to find out that there wasn't even a market.

Many people have had great ideas and never capitalized on them. Most never take any action at all. Fear controls them. They don't take the time to think or research enough to make an educated step forward.

> A first-time mistake is just a mistake.
> Repeating it is a decision.
> —Lori Grenier

Many entrepreneurs jump off that cliff and figure out how to build a plane on the way down. They just jump in and wonder why (the heck) they fell flat on their face. Too much excitement got the better of them.

Success can happen to anyone at any time, but having the ability to predict your success has nothing to do with luck. Some say one is "lucky to be good and good to be lucky"!

It's a bit misguided to think that you can time it. Success is a matter of learning what it takes to predict an eventual outcome.

How many times have you heard the saying, "Oh yeah, he was an overnight success!" or "He was very lucky!"? All I can say to that is *wrong*! I'm being nice. I could be using a different descriptive word. That is, in my opinion, in most cases, the furthest statement from the truth you are likely to ever hear.

Anyone who has ever achieved success in a large way, meaning that everyone takes notice, usually took a long time to do it. Most millionaires take over twenty years to accomplish that through trial and error. Most professional athletes played amateur sports for a decade before they ever got noticed.

Creating success takes time, perspiration, dedication, and stick-to-it-ness. It means they never, ever quit. You can't fail if you don't quit! Timing has little to do with it. You can, however, speed the process up! First, you need to make the decision to do something and then start. Second, you need to understand that you will likely fail from time to time. The faster you learn to make mistakes, the faster you will learn not to repeat them.

Most important, success is rarely achieved alone. Find a mentor. Find that driving force within you. Push yourself. Push your limits. Set goals, and miss them. Set goals, and break them. Set goals, and win.

Timing isn't everything, but it is something. Make the time to change, and your future will change. Allow yourself to change, and you will grow. True success comes from personal growth. You need to learn to grow. You cannot have a fixed mind-set, where you believe you have all the answers. You must have a growth mind-set. You must have the ability to accept change and grow. Learn from your mistakes. Invest in yourself first, and then invest in others. Success will only be a matter of time.

Secret Video #3

www.TheWealthPrinciple.net/chapter_three.html

Chapter 3

Are You Developing the Right Attitude?

The mind is like a parachute.
It doesn't work unless it's open.
—Unknown

Developing the right attitude and mind-set is an important ingredient to success as an entrepreneur. I spoke earlier about developing your ability to imprint on your subconscious mind to create the necessary habits and traits you need to be successful. But it starts with understanding a little bit about imprinting your mind-set.

The most important imprinting time in our lives was when we were children. Our early environment shaped how we think and act in our present lives today—most of the time, without us even knowing how or why we do the things we do.

For the longest time, I didn't really give it a second thought as to where I got my first imprinting or why I was so passionate about becoming a builder and developed an interest in becoming an author.

I remember when I was maybe four or five years old at the cottage, watching my dad, who was an RCMP by trade but decided he was going to build our cottage from scratch. I remember sitting in the background behind where he was building. I was sitting on a fallen tree pretending it was a car. I remember sitting there, watching him build the cottage. What I remember was he was framing the floor and starting to frame the walls. It took him a couple of seasons to build just the shell. But every day that I can remember, I would follow him down to the property and watch him build as I played. That was my first idea and look at construction. I was very young—at the age when you start imprinting, where some of your personality and interest traits are developed.

As I got older, I was always the kid who built the coolest tree forts. Out of all the kids at the cottage, I was the one who built all the tree forts! The one that stands out the most was the three-legged tree fort that had a trap door, screen walls, and a roof in a tree overhanging the lake. I built that fort, one of several, when I was only nine years old, all by myself. It was a cool place for all of us to hang out. Just another example of how I was imprinting on myself at an early age with the desire to build stuff.

Looking back at when I went to school, high school specifically, I remember my best class was my drafting class. Thinking back, I remember a time when I had to write a report for my drafting teacher. This is, I guess, when I had the first spark or an idea of writing stuff. I was given a task to write a report, not a book report, but an essay on a building project. So I wrote the essay on this project. I did all my research, and back then, everybody used *Collier's Encyclopedia*. I did all my research and wrote the report. I guess it was at a caliber that the teacher didn't quite believe that I had written this report. So he gave this report to my English teacher and asked the teacher if she believed that I could have written this. In my own defense, I had researched *Collier's*, and I did paraphrase. I didn't write word for word. I took what I read, and I rewrote it in my own words as best I could at that time. But you could tell that I had gotten the information from somewhere and that I was writing in a way that was completely different than anything else I had done. Even if you were to talk to me or looked at anything else I had written, it was like night and day the difference. The teachers gave me a passing grade because they couldn't say it was outright plagiarism. But my English teacher could tell that I had researched *Collier's* because she found the section I had researched. They both had a hard time believing that I wrote it. The reason I did so well on this essay was because I had a tremendous passion for what I was studying. I loved drafting and wanted to build stuff. At that time, I wanted to go to school to become a draftsman. I never ended up going to college or university. That's another story, but that's where I believe I got my first inklings of or I guess my ability to write. The reason I did so well was because I had a passion for what I wanted to do. And it started at a very young age.

When you start to understand how our minds work, you can start the process of change that is necessary for you to succeed. Several factors or traits come into play that you must become aware of. Your mind-set (we just spoke about imprinting), commitment, focus, passion, and confidence are part of a belief system that you need to develop for the right attitude to succeed.

We are all capable of change. Most of us don't like it because it sometimes contradicts what we learned when we were young. But you can change what you learned and reimprint and develop new habits that will impact your life in positive ways.

You will know that you have passion for what you want to achieve when you can recognize and see your own attitude change because of your focus and determination. You realize that your determination is happening without you consciously thinking about it. Passionate people don't just think; they do.

Passion can change your behavior.
—Gregory M. Luchak

Have you ever had the thought or idea that you might want to become an authority on a specific subject, learn a skill, or become an expert in your field? Maybe even become a public speaker, write books, or become a consultant, like I have?

I found that if you start using a voice recorder to record your personal thoughts and ideas and do that on a consistent basis that you can again imprint on your subconscious mind what you want to achieve consciously. You might be talking to yourself, thinking out loud, having private conversations. Try using a voice recorder. I found it easier to, for example, write this book by recording my personal thoughts and then transcribing them. I also found that I got more comfortable talking about the subject matter. Just so you know I didn't write the entire book this way. I used this method to discover and create content I put in this book.

This will give you the opportunity to train yourself not only to talk but to listen to how you talk. You can even go back, listen, and review. Make changes to how you think you should be sounding, and practice. You can do this anytime. You can do this while you're sitting at home or whenever you are alone. I'd say do it when you're driving in the car, but that could be tricky and dangerous. Absolutely don't do it while driving. Pull over to the side of the road or at a rest stop.

Don't lose the idea in your head. It may not come back to you later if you wait too long. You could be making these voice recordings when you're doing anything. I recorded a lot of my ideas for the book while I was cleaning the house or when I was painting on a job site somewhere. I'm always thinking. I have thoughts come into my head. I turn on the voice recorder as I'm working. As I'm doing whatever manual labor task, I'm talking about these ideas that come into my head. I learned to multitask and brainstorm while working, usually alone.

You'll find that you can start training your mind to think. You will start to make time for what is important and spend less time on meaningless tasks or other things, like watching TV. I often will have the TV on at night and just mute it. As I'm thinking, I'm writing, researching, or just doing tasks that I'm passionate about.

As human beings, as people, we have short attention spans. We can and do easily lose our train of thought. You may find as I did that I would often think or say something amazing in my head, or at least I personally thought was amazing. Maybe others wouldn't, but if you never write them down or talk out loud about them and make a voice recording, you'll never know if they were or not. Or you forget just what you were thinking and try to remember the exact details, and those ideas get lost in your subconscious until the day you hear someone else say or do what you thought about. Don't lose your train of thought. Make it a habit to record it. At least write it down.

I realized a long time ago that success does not really have a whole lot to do with financial wealth. A lot of people attribute success to wealth. They are connected, but having a bunch of money is not the only factor. In fact, it's a small factor in the equation.

In many ways, I started to recognize success principles in part from reading books, from trying to do stuff on my own. That's the biggest thing right there—trying to do things. I found that the only way to reach success was to overcome my fears and do the things that made me a little or even on occasion very uncomfortable.

I remember when I was in grade eight. We were given an assignment, and 50 percent of the mark was for doing a class presentation. I was literally petrified. In fact, I did the presentation, and the whole time I was up in front of the class, the only person I could look at was the teacher. So, I gave the presentation and started every sentence with "Miss Mahoney." I'm not even sure today if that was her name, but what I do remember was the entire class was laughing at me. At least it felt that way. I vowed I would never ever stand in front of a group of people again. And yet here I am writing a book, knowing full well that I will be standing in front of a group of people many times over. I realized the only way to reach success was to overcome my fears and do the things that made me a little or even on occasion very uncomfortable.

I am overcoming that fear because I am passionate about what I have learned and what I am teaching. I never thought I would be a teacher either—though I am more of a coach and mentor than simply a teacher. Teachers, for the most part, learn how to teach. They don't always necessarily have any experience with the subject matter. A coach and mentor, in contrast, typically teaches from experience. This is not a slight on teachers. You may be one, and a good one at that, but it isn't necessarily who I am.

> The major value in life is not what you get.
> The major value in life is what you become.
> —Jim Rohm

I developed the attitude that I would keep trying and keep going no matter what. And now you're wondering, can I do that too? Yes! You can!

What you do will speak so loudly that what you say sometimes nobody will hear. That is a version of a Napoleon Hill quote; I'm sure you have heard it at some point in your life.

Sometimes, you just need to do the things that you're thinking. People say, "OK, *you* can write a book. And because you wrote a book, people perceive you as having years of experience, giving you authority," which is a great reason why, I have learned, that a book is an awesome tool in marketing today. Books are the new business card. The process of writing this book has forced me to think a little harder about what I believe and what I can pass on as information and inspiration to you.

But now you're sitting there saying, "Well, I can't write a book!" Maybe you haven't got the experience yet, but I'm telling you that, yes, you can. But you first need to have a purpose and develop the passion for the idea. So again, back to passion—this is the driving force behind everything an entrepreneur does.

What do you have a passion for?

I believe that 90 percent of our success is to do with our character. The balance is our basic knowledge on a subject.

You never stop being an entrepreneur just because an idea failed. In fact, the process of failing forward is what most successful entrepreneurs go through. You try and try again. The more practice you get at performing a task, the more confidence you will have.

> Success isn't about what you read. It's about what you do!
> —Gregory M. Luchak

Unfortunately, most people will only try something new up to three times, believe they had no success, and quit. Failure is never an option. It is only a point in time that something didn't work out. Thomas Edison, who invented the light bulb, tried unsuccessfully about a thousand times to create the first light bulb. Imagine where we would be today if he quit after only three attempts. You fail. You pick yourself up, and you try again. You learn from the mistakes you made to improve the result. You will never get results until you try enough times. In the eyes of the entrepreneur, quitting is not an option. Ever!

The more practice you have, the more confidence you will have. Winning will also build your confidence. Have you ever seen a professional athlete or team quit? They play every game to the end with the prospect that they can win. They don't win every time. But they keep playing. They practice between games. They train in the off season. They study their opponents. They learn new skills. They create better habits. They seek the advice of a trainer and a coach, someone who has their best interest at heart and who can also see from a distance what steps they may be missing. The concept of winning is a team effort. Whether you are playing in an individual sport or as a group, success is best created in a team environment. Winning is only the result! The process of winning is what makes them successful.

I can tell you a story about when my son played hockey. He was playing with a team that was in a competitive double-A league. The coach, Greg McConnell, had a goal to position the team to place or win first or second in the league so that they could be invited to play in the provincial finals tournament. Typically, provincial finalists came from triple-A leagues. The coach's process was simple. Selecting the players for the team had very little to do with the individual ability or caliber of a player. Coach McConnell's first criterion was skating ability. His second criterion was coachability. This set the stage to teach and coach the players to play together as a team and learn to play a system of hockey that could position them to win. The result that year was the team ended up being undefeated in their league play. They only lost four or five games in tournament play, and as a caveat to the story, the coach only let the team play in Triple A tournaments. The team was invited to play in the provincials. They were the only team up to that point to ever go undefeated in the provincial tournament preliminary, semi- and quarter-final games.

The only game they lost was the gold medal game, which went into triple overtime before it was decided. It was a tremendous accomplishment. What made the team so good wasn't the individual play of any one player. The coach had very simple rules that everyone had to follow.

1. Practice three times a week.

2. If you don't have homework and want to hang out, only hang out with fellow players on the team.

3. Without exception, listen and follow the system the coach was teaching.

For a few players, listening to the coach was a challenge. They were either great puck handlers, goal scorers, or defenders. But the team had to learn to play together, know when to defend and when to go on offense. They had to learn how to follow leadership. Their ability to do that made them the best team that year and many other years. They were good players. None of them were exceptional, NHL caliber, I'd say. But they played like they were. They listened like they were. They had results like they were. None of the players ever made it to the NHL. A few played university or Junior A or Junior B. A couple played lower-tier professional hockey in the AHL and in Europe. They will all remember the season they had playing midget hockey and will never forget it. The lessons they learned have carried many of them far into their careers as leaders. I learned a valuable lesson from Coach Greg McConnell, watching how he transformed my son into a leader on the and off the ice.

Great leaders in life were first great followers. They studied and learned from mentorship. Great leaders practice and practice and keep trying whether they win, lose, or draw. They just never quit. They understand to position themselves to win, they need to get along with people. If you understand the lessons my son's hockey coach was teaching, you can understand why they were so successful.

Another trait successful entrepreneurs have is their ability to commit themselves 100 percent to a goal, challenge, or objective. As the following quote says, action brings your dream closer. When you commit to your dream, focus on the endeavor and have the belief that you can succeed. You will.

Commitment leads to action. Action brings your dream closer.
—Marcia Weider

Having read a lot of books and implemented the knowledge I have discovered, I know it is imperative that you develop personal habits that include your ability to focus, believe in yourself, and trust in others.

One of the exercises I learned was to meditate daily. It does take exercising your brain. In the beginning, it can be challenging. Just for an example, try not to think about anything for one minute. Don't let a single thought enter your mind. I will bet that the first time you try this, you will find that you are easily distracted. A noise, a flicker of light, or your imagination gets in the way of your ability to focus even for thirty seconds of your time.

What I learned was that you need to exercise your brain. Your brain is like a muscle. If you want to get better at memorizing stuff like people's names, events, and other information, you need to adapt the skills that reinforce your ability to do that. You need to spend time each day meditating so that you can learn to focus.

If you find you lack the ability to schedule your time to include time to meditate, start using a calendar. I use Gmail exclusively, not that I am endorsing it, but it's free and accessible from anywhere in the world that you can get an Internet connection. Start scheduling your time.

I found for myself that scheduling my time is a daily event. I usually do it every night. Reschedule and plan the weekly events and tasks, and carry that forward to long-term events and tasks for ninety-day intervals.

Now that you have started that process, lay out your daily activity. I don't really follow a set pattern as to when I meditate, read, write down my goals, or schedule my work activity. Most people schedule work activity during the day obviously. I usually start my day by doing the breakfast thing. Then the first task I do is write down my goals, which I repeat daily every day. If one of my goals had a time limit I missed, I reset the time limit (the date). Some may prefer to then take the next thirty minutes to meditate. Some do this at night as the last thing they do before bed, giving the impression that the last thing you think about may be the very things your subconscious dreams about. I'm not sure of the validity of that. That's your call. Some do it first thing in the morning as they get the impression that they start the day with a clear head. Spend some time every day meditating and planning your day, planning your life. You may waver from time to time, stopping or skipping a day, a week, or even a month between these tasks. You need to repeat this goal management process often. Focus is the key to your success.

So how do you physically meditate? Well, start by finding a quiet spot where you will have few distractions. Spend a few minutes just trying to focus on nothing at all. You will find this challenging. Ten seconds. Thirty seconds. One minute. It is not as easy as people think. It is the exercise of trying to stretch your mind to focus that is more important than how long you can do the exercise.

Always remember, your focus determines your reality.
—George Lucas

The next step is to learn to focus on an object. Pick anything in the room, and focus on that without letting any other thought or distraction in for the same amount of time—ten to sixty seconds. You follow that by thinking of one goal you want to achieve. Focus on nothing but that goal. What is it? How might you achieve it? When do you want to achieve it by?

Do those focus exercises for about fifteen minutes at a time. You will likely only spend about thirty minutes a day doing this. It does take practice and, like anything else, requires you to develop the habit daily for it to be effective.

Another ability you need to develop is handling stress. Focus and meditation will help, but ultimately you need to learn how to destress by eliminating the event that causes stress or prioritizing what is important in your life and will advance you toward your goal, not impede it.

I have often heard Dexter Yager speak about "majoring on the majors, not the minors."

"What's that about?" I'm sure you're asking. Many people have stress because of their financial circumstances, as an example. They constantly worry about the bills, having more month than money. Simply put—and you can extrapolate this to anything not just money as well—focus on tasks that will be the solution. Don't focus on the problem. When you are setting goals and tasks to reach your goal, your goal may be the solution you're looking for. You must focus on the task. The results of your actions will present the goal, creating the success, you're looking for. Sitting around worrying about a situation or a current negative result will never solve anything. Sometimes the best solution is to work, work toward that goal. Focus on the task that will get you there. The stress you have over a loss or potential loss will eliminate itself when you learn to focus on solutions rather than results. There will always be negative and positive results.

> Believe you can and you're halfway there.
> —Theodore Roosevelt

Do you believe? Believe in what you're thinking! When I talk about focus and acting to achieve your goal, the key ingredient is belief. If you don't believe in yourself, the idea, or even other people, you will never have success. Some call it blind faith. At the beginning of every day, you must believe that you can. Maybe you need to spend time with positive self-talk, reading positive books, listening to positive people. The biggest thing you need to do is to remove all negatives from around you. If a family member is negative toward you or your ideas, limit your contact with him or her. I state that because the number-one source of negativity often is family and then friends. Acquaintances and strangers really should have no impact on what you believe. You need to learn to ignore the negative. Again, focus on the positive.

Have belief in yourself. Have belief in your mentor. If you don't believe in the person you are following, why are you? And it may not be that person who has the problem. Oops! I'm not trying to offend anyone, but you should look at yourself first. Often, it is our fears that stand in our way. Or it is our lack of focus, our actions, and our belief system that are holding us back. You can fix it. I hope you now have some insight into how.

The answer isn't what's important;
The process to get there is.
—Robert Kiyosaki

Secret Video #4

www.TheWealthPrinciple.net/chapter_four.html

Chapter 4

Building Your Empire from the Ground Up

The Millennial Generation will prove to be the most
entrepreneurial generation of our time.
—Paul Zane Pilzer

We've talked about economics, passion, and purpose and how to unleash your entrepreneurial spirit, but I think it's important for you to know how to protect yourself from yourself. As an entrepreneur, you are going to make decisions. Sometimes, they will be good; sometimes, they won't. As you build your empire, you can be exposed to risk. To control the risk, you need to know how you can limit your exposure.

Over the course of my business career, I have owned different business entities. Some were Canada Corporations. Some were provincial corporations. I even used a trust agreement in one business deal to remain anonymous. I will be talking about both Canadian and American business structures. If you plan to span the borders, it's a good idea to know something about each country's options.

Your business structure is very important, especially if your plan is to become an independent business owner.

Asset protection is extremely important when building a business empire, whether you only plan to own a few businesses or properties or not. Most new investors and business owners don't realize the potential risk and financial harm they expose themselves to by not being properly protected.

In this chapter, I discuss forms of ownership and business structures to create asset protection and how to create liability protection through incorporation and the use of shareholder agreements and trusts. Start off with the right foundation to build your business from the ground up. Independent business ownership is what every big-thinking entrepreneur should be striving for.

There are several types of business formats that you can set up. Knowing how to manage and protect your business is extremely important to your success as an entrepreneur.

Operating strictly as a shareholder will afford you 100 percent liability protection and the freedom to control your time. Most business owners fall into the trap of their businesses controlling them. They invest most of their time operating the business when the idea of entrepreneurship is to spend your time being creative and putting teams of people to work for you. Creating a three-tier business structure will provide you the best asset protection system that you can create within a corporate structure.

Another reason to incorporate is to save money and profits from excessive taxation. Corporations are taxed differently than individuals. Personal income tax is based on your gross taxable earnings after your personal exemption is deducted. Depending on your level of income, you will be taxed federally and provincially combined on average 42 percent on all world income from all sources (anywhere from 10 percent on minimum taxable income to as high as 60 percent on a six-figure taxable income if you are filing as an individual). Literally, it will save you a huge percentage if you can operate through a corporation.

You will find that both Canada and the United States use the same term *world income*. Taxation can be a complicated thing to figure out. It is important to know that I am not a tax specialist or an accountant or a lawyer. You need to get everything I say here qualified from a professional, especially since laws can change, often with each new government administration.

As a self-employed business, you will be in the most vulnerable tax position. In many cases, this will cost you closer to 60 percent of your gross income as I stated earlier.

Visit the Canada Revenue Agency (CRA) and the Internal Revenue Service (IRS) to find tax rates that apply to your income, both personally and as a business.

Small-business Canadian controlled corporations (CCC) with sales under $5,000,000 are only taxed at 25 percent on net income after all expenses. The goal should be to keep most of your expenses allowable within the corporation. The income you receive personally as a dividend should be kept to a minimum, keeping your personal taxation below 20 percent. Depending on your desired lifestyle, you may be putting yourself in a higher personal tax bracket. That, of course, is your decision. It's extremely important to live a debt-free lifestyle personally. Keep the debt you choose to incur corporate where you have tax advantages.

As you can see, just based on the tax incentive alone, it pays to be an incorporated business owner and not to be employed by the competition! If you're self-employed, you are in competition on just about every level.

A sole proprietorship is a form of self-employment. You would be required to register with the CRA for a BN (business number). As a proprietor, you would be personally responsible for all liabilities and financial obligations. You would also be required to register for an HST account and a payroll account. Your tax account is your personal Social Insurance Number (SIN) account. Your business income is filed with your personal tax return. In Canada, if your main source of income is from construction, you would also be required to submit and file a Record of Contractor Payments (T5018 Reporting).

The advantage of operating as a proprietor is the low cost of start-up, ease of reporting, and having the least amount of government regulation and oversite. You would have direct control of all decision making. Any losses can be deducted from your other sources of income.

The disadvantage is you will have no liability protection. Your income will be subject to the highest tax brackets, as there is no cap.

The average self-employed person's tax accountability can be excessive and at a higher percentage of their earnings because they are considered employers and as such must contribute to the tax costs that employers are responsible for—such as, Canada Pension (CPP), employment insurance (EI), and in some cases, excise tax. In most cases, you will have little opportunity to manage your business from a distance. It is also the hardest form of business ownership in which to raise capital.

Partnerships are a type of business structure that have the same advantages and disadvantages as a proprietorship. You can protect yourself with a partnership agreement. You can also create a limited liability partnership where one partner provides financing or is responsible for debt obligations and the other partner is responsible for the management.

You should always use an independent lawyer to draw up an agreement that protects each partner's interest, establishing all the terms, such as division of profits and losses, how to handle dissolution, and conflict resolution and ensuring that the partnership meets all the legal requirements for a limited partnership.

The advantages are that start-up costs, assets, profits, and management can be shared. The tax advantage is that profits and losses can be applied to your personal income tax. The disadvantage is that each partner bears personal unlimited liability, and each can be held responsible for the business decisions made by either partner. Partnerships, however, can be difficult to operate. It is a challenge to find partners who are suitable for each other.

The process of incorporation is to create a legal entity that operates separately from shareholders. Corporations can be registered federally or provincially. Shareholders are not held personally liable for the debts, obligations, or acts of a corporation. Always seek legal advice before incorporating. It is easy today to set up a corporation online. However, if shareholders and investors are involved, an independent lawyer should create shareholder agreements, share structure, and any indentures the corporation will require. Any shareholder who is also an employee or a director can have some personal liability.

The advantage to incorporation is you can create limited liability, the ownership is transferable, there is business continuity, you have greater opportunity for tax advantages, it's a separate legal entity, and it is easier raising capital.

The disadvantages are that corporations are closely regulated and more expensive to operate and start up compared to proprietorships and partnerships; there are extensive regulatory filings, including shareholder and director meetings; and conflict resolutions and residency of shareholders and directors can be issues.

I discovered this next topic the hard way. I had a client with a warranty issue for a travertine bathroom floor. It was during a time when I had some financial difficulty. I couldn't find the time or the money to take care of it. My original mistake was not having a waiver on the tile, as it was garbage. But I accepted the responsibility, lack of waiver withstanding. The client, however, got impatient and was worried I would never follow through. They launched a small claims court action. Where I live, the process calls for a preliminary hearing, which they call a settlement conference. I had no problem with that. In fact, I told the judge that I wasn't there to argue the claim at all. By the time the hearing came along, I had the money to pay it. All was good until he wrote the judgment. You see, I was incorporated, a separate entity. He wrote the judgment against me personally. I asked him why. It made little difference, as I had planned to pay it anyway, but I wanted to know. The client was in fact a junior lawyer, and when she submitted the paperwork, she labeled me as a proprietary corporation. I looked for the term but couldn't find it anywhere. The judge said that he personalized the judgment to make sure that I, in fact, paid it. I decided I needed to research this further, and this is when I found in both Canada and the United States the term *personal service business*.[12] This can be a problem as well, considering your tax position. Whether you are considered an incorporated employee or self-employed, you may lose preferential tax treatment as well. You can be taxed as an individual rather than a corporation. In this case, I was at risk. I was identified as an incorporated employee and personally responsible for the liability. If you want to have personal liability protection, you must

[12] Canada Revenue Agency (CRA, 2016); Internal Revenue Service (IRS, 2016).

separate yourself from the day-to-day business activity. Businesses with five or fewer employees can be considered personal service businesses.

Financing usually comes with personal guarantees until the company is well established with a good track record. Directors can be at risk and subject to liability. Shareholders who are not employees or directors have 100 percent liability protection. Employees can be protected with a well-written contract between employees and the business and a contract between the business and its clients. Indemnification clauses should be written into every contract to protect employees and their heirs, heirs of directors, and any other heirs or representatives of the company. I also recommend a commercial liability insurance policy with at least $2,000,000 coverage. Real estate should have its own separate liability insurance policy. The fact is the only time you have 100 percent liability protection is when you are strictly a shareholder only. Take the following steps to ensure you limit yourself from liability.

1. Create a board of directors with stipulated functions.
2. Use business managers.
3. Have employees handle the day-to-day operations of the company. Have more than five employees.
4. Use a three-tier business structure.
5. Know that all directors of a company are personally liable for all Canada Revenue Agency source deductions and may be liable for other legal actions as well.
6. Carry liability insurance coverage.
7. Use a Shareholders Agreement.

Whether you own a business or are starting a new business, an assessment of the benefits and risks is required. You will want to put into place contractual arrangements to protect your interests. An agreement between two or more shareholders of a corporation or between the corporation and its shareholders can be used to manage the risks. This is a customized document and has stronger, more enforceable rules than standard corporate bylaws. It is normally used when shareholders are also directors or employees. A well-drafted agreement will have, in general, the following objectives:

- anticipation of likely as well unlikely events the corporation may encounter and how to deal with them, such as
  - changes in ownership and shareholder valuation
  - injection of additional capital
  - resolution of disputes
  - death of a shareholder or director
- management of the corporation
- determining voting rights and agreements
- a process for how shares will be transferred, including any restrictions
- dealing with the addition of new investors, shareholders, and directors
- rules for survivorship, how shares will be passed on
- maintenance of life insurance policies
- a list of the powers of the directors and supervision of the management team
- the business affairs of the corporation
- noncompetition rules
- rules for how to make, amend, or appeal bylaws
- remuneration of directors, including severance and bonuses
- limitations of directors with regards to issuing shares, borrowing money, making guarantees, security interests, banking, and so on
- indemnification of shareholders, directors, and other parties
- board representation, observer status, the nomination of directors
- quorum requirements at board and shareholder meetings
- amendments to the shareholder agreement
- exit alternatives for shareholders and directors

Efforts and courage are not enough without purpose and direction.
—John F. Kennedy

Under the Canada Corporations Act, a small business corporation can only have fifty or fewer shareholders. You are not allowed to solicit, advertise, or engage in mass media campaigns to promote the sale of shares. In any event, a prospectus of the company is required. A business with over fifty shareholders is required to meet extensive legal and Federal Trade Commission (FTC) requirements. You need to consult with a lawyer to have a proper shareholder agreement drafted. It is recommended that if you anticipate having more than one shareholder, you use a lawyer to incorporate. Although it is easy and inexpensive to incorporate online, it is a basic incorporation with standard bylaws and articles. Do your due diligence. Research the subject of incorporation. Similarly, the format of a shareholder agreement can also be used for a joint venture, partnership, or limited partnership agreement.

In Canada, the use of a three-tier business structure is the safest way to ensure the highest form of asset protection. This is accomplished by setting up a holding company that can be either a federal incorporation or a provincial incorporation. You can also use a trust instead of a holding company if you want to have certain tax advantages, such as the use of personal capital gains exemptions (currently $750,000 lifetime) that corporations are not entitled to. Keep in mind that trusts for this purpose can be very expensive to set up in comparison to incorporating. In today's dollars, you can set up a single incorporation online for from $650 to $900 online. You could hire a lawyer at a cost of $1,500 to $2,500. A trust in comparison could be as high as $10,000.

Your holding company then would incorporate an operating company that carries on the business activity only. Assets such as real estate or other business units can also be individually incorporated and owned by the holding company as well. All net income from these holdings are then passed onto the holding company as dividends tax free. The net cash assets from business operations can then be protected within the holding company and be reinvested or distributed to the shareholders. Shareholders can receive dividend income, leaving the major portion of taxable revenue in the corporation for future investments. The taxable revenue can be subject to tax somewhere between 15 percent and a ceiling of 25 percent, depending on how your accountant applies the rules. This is substantially lower than the higher rate you would pay as an individual. The idea would be to only draw a dividend or salary you require personally to live on, keeping your personal tax at the lowest rate possible. The key to this structure is not to hold assets personally and not to carry personal debt or liability. Keep yourself out of any possibility of a personal bankruptcy position. Your business assets can then be protected and your taxable income managed to maximize your profits. These are not loopholes, as some call them. They are legal tax rules that are to the benefit of businesses. Businesses create jobs, stimulating the economy to the benefit of everyone. The caveat is you need to be operating as a business to take advantage of them.

The holding company can be named or numbered. If the company is to use a name, you must obtain a name search to rule out any use of a name that is already taken. Articles and bylaws provide rules and regulations the corporation must follow. Generally, a corporation can have one director. A soliciting corporation must have a least three directors and appoint officers such as a president, secretary, and treasurer. A director can carry a term of up to four years. Any change to directors must be filed with Corporations Canada within fifteen days. Directors can be liable and held responsible for employees for up to two years following their term. Directors are also held accountable for any government withholding, such as HST and payroll. Amendments to the structure or number of directors must also be filed with Corporations Canada. Directors must be at least eighteen years of age, be individuals (real people), and not be declared incapable by a court of law or be bankrupt.

In a holding company, all assets are controlled by the company through the ownership in shares of each asset. Sometimes these assets can be referred to as business units or subsidiaries. All the net income from each business unit is passed up to the holding company as dividends, tax free. The holding company will pay tax on the overall net income of the company. There is no double taxation. As I mentioned earlier, a trust (a living trust or family trust) can be used instead of or in conjunction with a holding company. This is more of a tax-planning strategy. In Canada, we have a lifetime $750,000 capital gain exemption. This could change but for now is still in effect. When an asset is sold, the net proceeds are taxable. If you use a trust, each beneficiary can use his or her personal exemption collectively. If there are two or more beneficiaries, the taxable amount could be reduced further, as the proceeds are split per each beneficiary on a personal basis. This does not apply to a corporation. This is where you really need the advice of an accountant, as the holding company structure provides a lot of legal benefit. You may want to use a trust as well to retain the tax benefit if you are sharing your net worth with family as an example.

From an asset protection point of view, the holding company is strictly a shareholder-provided 100 percent liability protection under the law. The company, as a shareholder, can manage subsidiary companies by electing or by appointing a board of directors and managers who are employed directly with each individually owned company (asset). In the case of a three-tier structure, a separately held company can be used to employ the management team and carry out the general operations of the company. The team reports to the shareholders as mandated in the articles and bylaws of each company held.

The key thing to remember is that the holding company does not directly manage any asset or subsidiary. They are owned and controlled by the number of shares held. They are investments. Each asset is managed by its own individual directors and employees. As the shareholder, the holding company has the right to hire, appoint, or fire the individual board of directors with their controlling interests in share ownership that carry voting rights. As a shareholder, you can be a director or an officer employed by any of the companies held within the ownership structure. However, this will reduce your personal as well as corporate liability protection. The key to liability protection is separation.

The basis of using a three-tier system is to separate the ownership of each asset by its individual purpose, keeping the management and employees separate from each real property in a non-asset-bearing company. A real property can be described as real estate or a business that includes tangible assets that can be sold. The holding company invests capital into each asset and nonasset property and receives dividends in return. If the operating company runs into a legal problem, there are no assets held in the company or at risk. If an asset-bearing company runs into trouble, the holding company has the option to reorganize the management and refinance or sell the asset with full liability protection to itself and any other companies it owns.

If you are just starting out in business and you plan to be a part of the operations of any of your companies, you will not be at arm's length. You can only remain at arm's length if you are strictly a shareholder. Non-arm's length would mean direct or indirect involvement in the day-to-day operations of the subsidiary company invested. The key is to use a management team and keep everything separated by share ownership. In the beginning, most business owners are shareholders, directors, officers, and employees. The key is to separate yourself as much as possible. This is how you become an independent business owner.

To set up your first corporation or a holding company structure, you should hire a lawyer. If you intend to register these companies online, which is easy to do, you may in the future need to file amendments, as your operating structure will likely change as your business scales up. You will likely elect and appoint directors and officers as required. You may have to amend the bylaws to reflect your ability to do this. If you plan to have management from the very beginning and not be directly employed, then you will absolutely need a lawyer to file the correct bylaws and articles. In any case, you should consult a lawyer and an accountant.

There are three main entities that most investors use in the United States: C corporations, S corporations, and limited liability companies (LLC). A holding company structure can be used in the United States as well. A famous one you would recognize is Warren Buffet's Berkshire Hathaway. The same strategy I outlined earlier, a three-tier business structure, can be used in the United States as well, creating asset protection for a single person as well as corporate asset protection.

C corporations are designed for high-income producers. The corporation is taxed as a corporation, and any salaries paid out to shareholders are taxed as income on your personal tax return. This is double taxation and not the best form of incorporating for real estate as an example. Annual filings with the state and annual meetings are required and have to be documented.

S corporations are not subject to double taxation, and dividends are exempt from Social Security taxation if the owners are paid a reasonable salary, an important feature if you plan to flip property as opposed to use it for rental income, which would be subject to Social Security tax at an estimated 15 percent, plus the applicable taxation on income.

S corporations are not allowed to have non-US residents and are restricted to seventy-five shareholders and to 80 percent ownership of another corporation. Annual filings and annual meetings are required and have to be documented. Therefore, Canadians are not allowed to own or operate these types of corporations.

Limited liability corporations (LLCs) are designed to provide the limited liability of a corporation and the flexibility of a partnership and are taxed as a sole proprietor or as a corporation. They are also favorable to capital gains tax rates and depreciation and can be exchanged for other real property tax free (1031 exchange). Filing and setting up an LLC is generally simpler and less costly than setting up a C corporation.

LLCs also allow pass-through tax and can reflect on a personal tax return as income or loss for the owner(s). An unlimited number of members (owners) are allowed. Non-US residents are also allowed. LLCs can have subsidiaries without restriction. LLCs usually have limited life spans. A dissolution date is often required in its articles.

Annual meetings are not required, but all decisions made should be recorded and documented and members should be notified.

Canadians can own LLCs; however, there may be immigration rules to follow. You can own and manage an LLC from outside the country but are not allowed to draw a salary or be employed in the LLC. You can travel to the United States on a B1 or B2 visa as a business visitor. While in the United States as a business visitor, you can conduct negotiations, solicit sales, invest, discuss purchases, attend meetings, interview staff, and conduct research. You cannot, however, run the business day to day or have "gainful employment." These require a different immigration status, such as an H1B visa or green card. The maximum visitation allowable with a B1 or B2 visa is one year. Generally, up to six months is granted upon entry. For longer periods, you should apply in advance, and they can take several weeks to receive. You may also have to prove that you are a Canadian resident with a legal address and that you intend to return, proof could be having a Canadian source of income or gainful employment in Canada. This may give you the answer to why you are asked certain questions at the US border if you have ever crossed by car or passed through immigration at a US airport terminal.

Based on my current research, the most widely used LLC is a Delaware LLC. It has been stated that they are the best state in which to incorporate a start-up, as they have favorable laws for corporate governance. State laws favor companies that don't do business in the state. They can also easily be converted to a C-corp with one state filing and one IRS filing. Delaware is a great base to start a business from, as evident by the 1,000,000 plus companies that have registered there but in fact don't conduct business in the state. They only require an annual franchise fee of $200. The other requirement is to have an agent represent you, which starts around $99 and goes up, depending on the services they provide you. Any dividends you earn as the owner are passed through tax free to your personal tax return, based on your residency. The key word here is *residency*. You only pay tax in the country you reside in.

Therefore, your immigration status is important. You can only travel, for example, to the United States as a visitor between four and six months a year, based on an immigration travel calculation. If you exceed the allowable time frame, you must declare your residency. You may have to remain in Canada to not exceed the limits; otherwise, you must file a US tax return, where you must declare your world income and may have to pay up to 30 percent in withholding taxes on income earned in the United States. You may also have to file a Canadian tax return and report on your world income as well. There is a treaty between our countries that allows a claim for a foreign tax credit offsetting the tax. But this can be complicated, depending on how business is conducted and reported. In either case, if you exceed the immigration rule or you are seen to consistently be crossing our borders frequently, you will raise red flags and be questioned as to what you are doing. It may appear that you are violating residency or employment rules. You may have to apply for the appropriate visa before you enter the United States for business purposes.

Nevada LLCs are widely used by real estate investors to provide liability protection and anonymity. The state of Nevada adds extra privacy because investors are not required to appear on the state records as an officer of the company. Investors can use a Nevada LLC as trustee to keep their name out of the public records. In combination with a trust agreement, this creates asset protection. They can be owned and used in all fifty states.

To fully understand the tax implications between these forms of incorporation, contact a US and Canadian tax advisor before you conduct any business in the United States. The same is true for Americans who want to invest in Canada, especially now that the dollar is more favorable to Americans than Canadians.

Never give up on what you really want to do.
The person with big dreams is more powerful
than one with all the facts.
—Albert Einstein

Secret Video #5

www.TheWealthPrinciple.net/chapter_five.html

Chapter 5

Shaking the Money Tree

When you know what you want,
and you want it bad enough,
you will find a way to get it.
—Jim Rohm

Are you looking for that money tree to shake? You are only limited by your imagination and your ability to understand, negotiate, and finance a deal. I need to say that you should be very careful financing your business ventures. Risk in today's economic conditions is highly scrutinized by the banks, brokers, and any potential lender. Many gurus tout that you should always use OPM (other people's money) not your own. Today, that is a highly dubious endeavor. The recent financial turmoil we witnessed in the United States from 2008 through 2012 sent fear around the world.

My caveat here is to warn you that OPM is great, but you need to understand risk and the unnecessary position that many businesspeople and investors put themselves in because of their lack of financial knowledge.

In this chapter, I discuss credit bureaus and bankruptcy, among other topics. The reason I decided to include this information, from a personal note, is because I have experienced situations where I needed the information. You may not require the information personally, but you very likely know someone who does. If you get into real estate investing, you absolutely can use this knowledge to help people.

Many investors went bankrupt because of poorly negotiated highly leveraged mortgage products. In the United States, it was very easy to find lenders with whom you could overleverage a deal with very little scrutiny on the borrower. Some refer to these as *ninja loans*—no interest, no job applications. These high-risk, high-reward lending practices eventually led to the collapse of the markets.

In Canada, however, it is extremely hard to do this, as you will find that many lenders will ask, "How much skin do you have in the game?" meaning you must have some money of your own in the deal, and often they won't lend in most instances for business purposes, including real estate, more than 80 percent. In most cases, you need to show where your cash is and how long it has been held there as proof that it is yours to use. It can be tricky if you plan to use a silent partner as your source of capital.

In the case of a business, it may only be 60 percent, and they will only lend based on what the business can afford. Whether you're borrowing money for a business or commercial property, lenders will look at the debt-coverage ratio. They are usually looking for a 1.2 ratio or better. Lenders want to see a profit margin—typically, 20 percent after debt servicing. You can secondary finance; however, the numbers, at the end of the day, must work.

Simply put, if you're starting out in business or real estate and you don't have any skin in the game, find a partner who has the money. Find and use the techniques I teach in my program to your advantage to create capital without risk or at least limit the risk to a manageable level. Leverage your knowledge and expertise.

Once you begin to build capital of your own, you will find it simple in comparison to leveraging a deal that will work with OPM. Having said all that, I encourage you to learn to be creative.

There are many ways to finance property or a business. Most only know of one or two—going to a bank or a mortgage broker. In real estate, you can find a bank, be the bank, have the seller be the bank, or even sell the bank.

When I talk to people looking for financial solutions, I recommend some simple techniques to use.

First, if your plan is to apply for financing, for instance on a real estate deal, I recommend that you use a mortgage broker and not go directly to a bank.

Brokers will only hit your credit once, whereas if you travel from bank to bank, you will get multiple hits that could affect your credit score. You may appear as a credit seeker, even though you are an investor.

Here is another quick story of how I learned this lesson the hard way. If you go the bank route and that bank turns your application down, all other branches within that bank's control will also turn you down. Back in the day, you had the opportunity to deal with a bank manager. But they recorded all the applications within the bank's global system. Today, it's all computerized and analyzed by machine, and there is no way to get around the system by knowing one easy bank manager over someone who isn't. Using a broker is an easier way to find a lender than going directly to an institution.

If you are borrowing from family and friends, you need to be aware of the difference between what is arm's length and non-arm's length. Non-arm's length is when there is a close relationship between two parties, such as family members, or for example an internal relationship between shareholders or a parent company and a subsidiary.

Many loans and mortgages can also be government guaranteed. Another source I recommend is to find a lawyer who specializes in private financing.

I have always been very interested in and focused on real estate investing. It was an early passion of mine, and I learned this next technique completely by accident. The ultimate lender you should always look for is of course the seller. The seller will always be the least interested in the academics of lending and more prone to making a deal.

Understanding what I just referred to is basically learn and understand what "notes" are. Notes are the actual legal document describing the lending agreement. You can in some instances assume the note; you can create the note and then sell the note, have the seller create a note, have the seller sell the note, or even sell part of that note for capital or cash flow for yourself or the seller. Notes are simply instruments that identify a loan that is then registered against real property as a lien or mortgage. The real property is the collateral. Such property could be a car, a boat, an RV, precious metals, jewelry, inventory, or even sales invoices.

As for understanding the basics of borrowing, the cost of a loan, mortgage, trust, or promissory note can be calculated with simple or compound interest. They can be interest only or principal and interest. They can be set out with a predetermined length called the "term" that the current interest rate will be applied to. When the term has expired, the loan can be renegotiated or paid out based on the outstanding balance. The amortization schedule describes the total amount of payments to be applied on a monthly, bimonthly, and semiannual basis, or balloon payment over the life of the loan. A loan can also include conditions, such as nontransferable, assumable, assumable with approval, or nonassumable. They can include penalties for paying off prior to the term expiring, such as three months' interest. They usually call for the requirement of insurance and the payment of property taxes on a monthly or annual basis.

Mortgages require a lawyer to draft and register the document with the land registry office. Other conditions also outline rules in case of default. In Canada, some provinces are *power of sale*, meaning they are nonjudicial, and some are judicial, meaning the court will rule on the process of foreclosure.

The property loan process in the United States does differ from state to state. Some states use *land trusts*, and some use mortgages. Some states allow nonresident ownership. Some have caveats, such as the state of California. If you are from another country, for example, you may own real estate, but it is nontransferable upon death, meaning that you either must sell it before you die, or it goes back to the state upon your death. I don't believe this rule has changed. Always research and understand the rules of the jurisdiction you are buying and borrowing in.

Other rules you should be aware of are caveats such as due-on-sale clauses. If a property sells and you wish to have the loan, mortgage, or promissory note be assumable, it may be written into the agreement that the full balance is due and payable upon the sale or transfer of the property. Virtually all institutional lenders have this clause. This makes it difficult for an investor wanting to keep the existing financing in place.

In 1982, the US Congress passed the Garn–St. Germain Depository Institutions Act, making it federal law. In Canada, most lenders have the right to approve the new buyer prior to the transfer.

If you are wanting to be creative and possibly use someone else's credit or loan, you need to really study how you can control a property without actually having title to the property.

Trust agreements, partnerships, and even the jurisdiction you use to structure your deal can make a difference in how you creatively finance your deal. The area of law is vast. Even the most astute lawyer does not know every aspect of the law.

Through research, I discovered various techniques to finance. I even had to teach my lawyer a few of them that he had no idea either existed or were even legal until he checked them out. Study up. Don't just rely on what I have written here. Google it! Yahoo it! Think out of the box!

Your credit and, more important, the credit of your tenants, buyers, and customers are a constant issue. You can operate without credit for a limited time, but if your credit is damaged, you will need to repair it at some point to move forward in your business career. Knowing how to repair credit and the pitfalls is essential to helping people with their credit. Building good relationships by helping people will build your business. Becoming a financial problem solver starts with you.

You may be asking what makes me an expert. I'm not. But I have had just about every credit problem any one person could ever have during the past thirty plus years in business—bank account seizures, Canada Revenue examinations, Worker's Safety Insurance Board (WSIB) audits, seizures, and bankruptcy. Twice. That's right! I learn the hard way. I hope you don't. I can tell you that I am not alone. Many people, including a lot of people you know, have credit issues. They just don't want to talk about it.

There are several options available to people with challenged credit. They can try to negotiate with creditors personally, although this can be tough; they can seek professional help with a credit counselor or a hire a trustee in bankruptcy. Credit counselors can negotiate on their behalf with creditors. They can also file a credit proposal with the superintendent of bankruptcy. A trustee can represent a bankruptcy and file on behalf of a bankrupt entity, but they represent and act in the interest of the creditors, not the bankrupt party.

There are two main credit reporting agencies, Equifax and Trans Union. Plus, in some cities, there are local credit bureaus. Trans Union is a Canadian company with offices in Hamilton, Ontario. Equifax is an American company, located in Georgia, with offices in Montreal, Quebec. Inquiries into your report remain on file for three years. Bankruptcy remains on file for seven years from the date of discharge or assignment, depending on the circumstances of the bankruptcy. A second bankruptcy can remain on file for fourteen years. Credit proposals remain on file for a period of three years from the date of the final debt settlement.

Credit ratings are established by measuring the payment history (at 35 percent), the credit history (at 15 percent), types of credit used (at 10 percent), new credit (at 10 percent), and the amounts owed (at 30 percent). Credit scoring uses a mathematical formula. The higher the score, the better the credit report is. The current system being used was created by the Fair Isaac Company. Equifax refers to this scoring system as the FICO score. Trans Union refers to this score as the empirical score. Others refer to credit scoring as the beacon score. Credit ratings are posted using an alpha numeric system ranging from R0 to R9. R stands for "revolving credit" and I for "installment loans." Payment history includes payment information, public records, collection agency records, and amounts owed. Credit history includes how long your accounts have been established and how long since you used these accounts. New credit includes how long it has been since you opened a new account, how many new accounts you have, how many recent requests you have made, and the length of time since inquiries have been made on your account. Types of credit include revolving lines of credit, fixed loans, and credit cards.

Credit Scoring ranges from 0 to 900. The average is between 400 and 850. Scores above 680 used to be ideal. Since the banking scare in 2007–2008, credit has become harder to get. Where high-net-worth individuals used to easily get institutional financing, now they are having to go to the private lending market, making it difficult for small investors to find private lenders through mortgage brokers. High-net-worth investors are usually accredited investors with $1 million in net worth. Now scores above 750 are ideal. Scores between 680 and 750 are scrutinized more closely. Scores between 620 and 680 are considered high risk, and any score below 620 likely will not be approved for any type of financing. It is important to check both main reporting agencies. Often the information is different between them, as creditors have a preference as to whom they report to first. Outstanding balances on loans may be incorrect. Tax liens and judgments may not appear and may not have reported the payment or discharge. Check your credit with both agencies to ensure they are correct and up to date.

Credit Ratings	Explanation
R0	The loan is too new, has been approved but not used yet.
R1	The loan was paid within thirty days; no payments were overdue.
R2	The loan was paid after thirty days; no more than two payments were overdue.
R3	The loan was paid after sixty days; no more than three payments were overdue.
R4	The loan was paid after ninety days; no more than four payments were overdue.
R5	The loan is 120 days overdue, and no payments have been made.
R6	The loan is 150 days overdue, and no payment arrangements have been made.
R7	The loan is repaid through credit counseling.
R8	The loan is repaid through repossession of merchandise, chattels, sale of assets.
R9	The loan is now bad debt and has been placed into collection.

> If you find yourself in a hole—
> the first thing you should do is stop digging.
> —Will Rogers

It is important to have a good credit report if you intend to borrow money from lenders through a bank or mortgage broker, as they always check your credit before lending. You will also find that insurance companies, landlords, utility companies, telephone companies, and many other agencies now check your credit before you can use their services. Even the worst credit can be repaired if you follow a few basic principles and establish a trend of good credit practices.

The following are strategies you can use to improve your credit score and credit rating.

- Contact your creditors. Explain why you can't make payments. Suggest making lower payments. Try to get a new payment plan approved.
- Credit-counseling services are provided by counseling agencies and associations found in many cities. They can help you create a budget and negotiate a payment plan on your behalf.
- You can obtain a debt consolidation loan from your bank. Be sure to stop using your revolving credit until the consolidation loan is repaid.
- A consumer proposal can be made under the Bankruptcy and Insolvent Act. Like credit counseling, a trustee can apply to the court to reduce the outstanding principal and create an installment plan for the creditors.

Once you have paid down your credit, you need to establish good credit practices:

- Never use your full credit available.
- If you have a $5,000 credit card, only use $2,500 and pay it off monthly.
- If you have installment loans, double up your payments or make annual lump sum payments to pay them off early.
- Apply for credit when you don't need it, and pay it off quickly.
- Don't apply for credit at multiple agencies at the same time, as you will appear to be a credit seeker.
- Use a mortgage broker, as they will only check your credit once during the application process, even though they may be applying to several lenders at the same time to find one that will give you acceptable terms and conditions.
- Stop using unnecessary credit, such as store credit, multiple credit cards, lines of credit for personal use, vehicle loans, or leases for personal use.

- Only use credit for business purposes, so you can write off the interest expense. Any credit used for personal use is a bad credit practice.
- Learn to save or use profits to buy personal items and luxuries. A large trend today is the use of branded credit cards from big box stores and grocery stores to collect points enticing you to buy more everyday stuff on credit. Everyday living expenses should always be paid in cash, not with credit.
- Be aware of how you use credit.

The process of paying off debt can be daunting and requires discipline. To start with, you need to know what your spending habits are. Do this by tracking everything you spend on a daily, weekly, and monthly basis. You need to figure out what your discretionary spending compared to your nondiscretionary spending is. Calculate how much you earn versus how much you spend. Is there any surplus? How much do you spend on debt servicing? The following is an example of how you can pay down debt quickly with some discipline.

My Get-out-of-Debt Strategy

1. Prioritize your debt per the outstanding balance from smallest to largest and the minimum monthly payment.
2. Calculate how much debt service you can afford to pay— usually about 30 percent of your net income. If you have surplus income, add that to the amount you generally would pay toward debt.
3. Apply the surplus income to the smallest amount owing, the idea being that you pay that debt off as quickly as possible.
4. When you have paid the smallest debt owing, apply the surplus income plus the amount you were paying to the paid-off debt and add that amount to the next smallest debt outstanding.
5. Repeat the process until you have only one debt left. Now you can apply the entire 30 percent debt service amount plus all the surplus to that debt until it is paid off.

The example shown in table 2 demonstrates how you can pay off $36,000 in approximately forty months by applying $200 of surplus income to the existing minimum payments and then systematically adding the net surplus to the next outstanding debt payment. If you only apply the minimum payment, it would take sixty months (five years of your life) to pay off all the debt. You can save twenty months of time, payments, and interest.

Table 2: Debt Reduction Example

Example	Minimum Payment	Outstanding Principal	Monthly Surplus	Total Monthly Payment Applied	Acc. Months to Pay Off
28% Store Credit	$41	$1,000	$200	$241	5
19% Credit Card	$150	$5,000	$241	$391	21
7% Line of Credit	$150	$5000	$391	$541	26
8% Car Loan	$500	$25000	$530	$1,041	40
Total	$841	$36,000	$200	$1,041	40

This example shows how you can pay out $1,041 per month for forty months for a total payout of $41,640 to pay off $36,000 in principal. The interest savings alone works out to about $3,000.

Anyone who has never made a mistake has never tried anything new.
—Albert Einstein

This next section discusses how bankruptcy works. Bankruptcy is a legal process, regulated by the superintendent of bankruptcy (OSB),[13] that may allow people to be discharged from most of their debt. When people declare bankruptcy, their assets are given to a trustee in bankruptcy, who then sells them and distributes the proceeds

---

[13] *Superintendent of Bankruptcy,* (Government of Canada)
 www.ic.gc.ca/eic/site/bsf-osb.nsf/eng/home
 United States Trustee Program. (Wikipedia)
 https://en.wikipedia.org/wiki/United_States_Trustee_Program

among the registered creditors. Once bankruptcy has been declared, unsecured creditors cannot take legal steps to recover their debts, such as seizing assets or garnishing wages. Creditors in some cases can pursue the bankrupt after the discharge date. Once people are legally bankrupt, they are required to perform certain duties, such as delivering all the property that is in their possession or control, such as credit cards, books, records, documents, insurance policies, and tax returns and attend before an official receiver for examination under oath with respect to their conduct and the causes of the bankruptcy and the disposition of their property. A statement of affairs will be drawn up within five days and registered with the court. The bankrupt will also have to submit a prebankruptcy tax return and a post-bankruptcy tax return. If it is the first bankruptcy, they will be automatically discharged after nine months if they have no surplus income. If they have surplus income, the discharge will occur after twenty-one months. If it is a second bankruptcy, they will be automatically discharged after twenty-four months if they have no surplus income. If they have surplus income, it will be thirty-six months before being discharged.

The bankruptcy will stay on credit reports for a period of seven years following the date of discharge. Bankrupts with personal income tax debt over $200,000 or more, representing 75 percent or more of personal debt, are not eligible for an automatic discharge. Discharge only happens if no opposition to the discharge has been given to the superintendent of bankruptcy. Once a discharge has been given, the bankrupt is released from most debts. Any debts that arise out of damages for any criminal act, alimony, child support, fraud, or student loans are not released. A judge can order an absolute discharge, conditional discharge, or suspended discharge. The cost of bankruptcy is outlined by the superintendent of bankruptcy. The superintendent of bankruptcy standards can be found by visiting their website.[14]

Typical fees are $200 per month for twelve months for first-time bankrupts, $200 per month for twenty-four months for second-

---

[14] *Superintendent of Bankruptcy,* (Government of Canada)
www.ic.gc.ca/eic/site/bsf-osb.nsf/eng/home

time bankrupts, and $7,500 for corporate bankruptcy. Any surplus income prior to the discharge must be turned over to the trustee. Guidelines regulating the calculation of surplus income are available on the OSB's website.

A bankrupt is entitled to keep certain personal items as regulated by the superintendent of bankruptcy.[15] The following are currently what is allowed:

Allowable Equity

Vehicle $5,650

Household Goods $11,300

Tools of Trade $11,300

Farmers $28,300

Home $0

Clothing $5,600

RRSPs are exempt and protected from bankruptcy, provided the amount has been invested for a period longer than twelve months. Any money that was paid out in the previous twelve months and up to thirty-six months following the date of bankruptcy that is considered surplus can be clawed back, payable to the estate of the bankrupt.

Another note on RRSPs and specifically "locked-in plans," sometimes called LIRAs or RIFs. These plans, if they are registered federal plans, can be unlocked under financial hardship rules. The financial institution will have the appropriate documentation to administer this type of transaction. Be aware that if this is done post-bankruptcy, rules apply to the amount of income an individual or a family can earn. Guidelines are set out in the bankruptcy act. Do some

---

[15] *Superintendent of Bankruptcy*, (Government of Canada) www.ic.gc.ca/eic/site/bsf-osb.nsf/eng/home

research. The trustee will determine what the surplus income based on these rules is, if any.

A trustee in bankruptcy is an officer of the court who administrates the bankruptcy but is acting on behalf of creditors, not the bankrupt. A bankrupt is required by law to disclose to any creditor in advance or by application that he or she has been bankrupt. Not disclosing that fact is an offense and can carry fines up to $5,000 and/or three years in jail.

A note on corporate bankruptcy and personal responsibility— all directors of a corporation are personally liable for any government source deductions, such as harmonized sales tax (HST) or payroll deductions. If a company is in default with the Canada Revenue Agency on either of these and the corporation declares bankruptcy, the debt will follow the directors personally. In any event, the debt is not covered by personal or corporate bankruptcy. The debt will survive. A personal bankrupt is not allowed to be a director during his or her bankruptcy period. At the end of his or her bankruptcy and discharge, he or she can still be held accountable for the corporate source deduction debt, especially if he or she plans to activate the corporation or conduct business with the corporation in the future. The trustee will not undertake any action for a corporation on behalf of a personal bankruptcy. The trustee will seize the corporate assets and shares and sell them. Upon discharge, the bankrupt can technically reinstate as a director and begin corporate activity again at a risk of being held accountable for the debt. Corporate bankruptcy is a separate action. Often personal bankrupts who were directors and shareholders do not pay for a corporate bankruptcy. They walk away. Seek legal advice in this event.

I will sum up this chapter and keep it simple. The secret to shaking the money tree is to first bootstrap your business. Create profit and capital with your business. Go out and earn it. Lenders will come knocking, not the other way around.

If you want options,
Become an entrepreneur,
Build a business, Invest in real estate.
Start part-time. Do it in your Spare-time.
—Gregory M. Luchak

Secret Video #6

www.TheWealthPrinciple.net/chapter_six.html

Chapter 6
Strategy! Strategy! Strategy!

The only impossible journey is the one you never begin.
—Tony Robbins

I struggled a bit with just how much information I was going to include here. This chapter reveals real estate strategies anyone can use. I literally could write an entire book on real estate investing. Well, actually, I did. I wrote an entire course, the release of which will follow this book. For now, I am going to give you the secret to five basic strategies, four of which I personally have used.

First and foremost, there are no legitimate get-rich-quick schemes. Except if you were to compare working as an employee for your entire life to owning a business. As I have heard Warren Buffet say more than once, the principle of compound interest is a marvelous thing. But I would also say that learning to have patience to let it work is the key. Most don't comprehend how that really works. Creating value in a business from start-up to full potential, buying an undervalued business and fixing it, or investing in real estate is a process that takes time. Time can be a magical thing when you let it work for you. Having said that, you can become wealthy by investing over time, making sound investment decisions based on practical knowledge and strategies.

A pessimist sees the difficulty in every opportunity.
An optimist sees the opportunity in every difficulty.
—Sir Winston Churchill

I like how real estate works. It has worked for me on numerous occasions. As an example of how wealth can be created, I have learned a thing or two I can share. Investing in real estate can be done in a multitude of ways with all kinds of property. However, when you get right down to it, there are only five basic entry-level and exit strategies.

The most common, as everyone has seen on TV, is rehabbing, commonly known as "flipping." The reality is you can rehab and flip, rehab and hold, or buy and hold. You can *wholesale* a deal as well as *lease option* a property.

There are three questions you need to answer: what, how, and when? The key to a good deal is to first know what it is you are buying and how you are going to pay for the purchase. You need to decide on how long you plan to hold the property and when you plan to sell it. If you have no capital and have no connections to lenders or partners, then the opportunity may exist for you to wholesale or use lease options.

My Real Business Investors Software is a program I designed to create a purchase plan using one of these strategies by implementing the knowledge from this book and My Greatest Business and Investor Training Program is a seminar series I developed to go along with the software program.

To start, you should never have real estate holdings of any kind in your personal name, with exception of your personal residence. In the training program, I discuss in detail contracts, marketing, and how and when to make offers, plus a lot more. Today, I will give you some tips and strategies to wet your tongue with.

Business is all about "the art of the deal." Now some of you may be saying that I am stealing Donald Trump's famous title. The fact is business is about the art of making deals, and Trump doesn't own that exclusivity. True businesspeople relish the opportunity to make a deal work. It is the drug, if you will, of the entrepreneur. The more deals, the better. The bigger the deal, even better! Whether you're buying a business or any income-producing asset, like real estate, your ability to negotiate is critical to your success.

This section discusses the business of real estate investing, the types of strategies, and how you can make money with them. So, taking that into account, I am going to give you some pointers on what to look for in an opportunity and how to negotiate deals.

The fact is you need to understand from all sides what is and can be involved in a deal that you can exploit. I don't like to use that word, but that is exactly what you will be doing. The point I should make, having said that, is even though you are looking to exploit a situation, keep in mind that we are always dealing with people. People make emotional decisions, not necessarily logical decisions. In either case, all parties to a deal must feel (emotion) that they can win with your proposal. You have heard the term *win-win*? It is a fact.

Creating a great business deal is about finding opportunity by solving a problem. It could be on many levels. With real estate, the problem to solve often, if not always, is financial. Someone needs to sell a property. The issue could be the seller is in financial distress. The property may need significant repairs they can't afford. Maybe it's an estate sale, and the family want a quick sale. Maybe they hate being landlords. There is always a reason. Your job is to find the reason and provide a solution that both you and the seller can benefit from.

The first real estate seminar I ever attended, back in 1985, was Tom Vu's How to Buy Real Estate. I never forgot this training because to this day it is one of the very few that was worth every penny. If memory serves me, it was $150 for a one-day, twelve-hour course. The premise was—you got it—find a problem and solve it. The training that I found to be most important was the technique they taught on how to negotiate a realistic price on a property that a seller could not ignore.

The strategies I talk about when investing in real estate typically expect you to look for property or owners who are in some way in distress. The points of negotiation that I relate to are best used directly with a seller. Dealing with agents in most cases yields next to no results because an agent for the seller is working on behalf of the seller's best interests. They only want to see the bottom-line offer. If you are perceived as low-balling (a term used to throw a low offer as bait), they will likely instruct the seller to ignore you or counter at their full price.

The potential for negotiating a deal in your favor lies with your ability to deal directly with the decision maker. Typically, the best deals never get to an agent. You need to do some legwork to find a seller before he or she lists with an agent. To start, you need to recognize distressed property or the distressed owner. The easy properties to spot are *tall-grass* properties. They are usually vacant, physically run-down properties. If you're looking for income-producing property, you may want to look for landlords who are looking to retire. The use of bird dogs is an important strategy for a real estate investor. Consult property managers, lawyers, credit counselors, trustees, and even the classifieds to find FSBO (for sale by owners) estate-sale notices. The point is you need to go out and find a deal. Find out who the owner is and send him or her a letter of intention.

Now how do you negotiate with a seller? First and foremost, find out what he or she wants. You need to have a conversation to find the root of the problem. You can't provide a solution unless you know what it is, especially if the problem is financial. Maybe it's a pending divorce, a job loss, late mortgage payments, or a partner who wants out. Once you know, then you can start looking at the numbers. The numbers need to work. Period. Business is about numbers. It is not emotional. But people make emotional decisions. To succeed, you have to be the logical negotiator in the deal. From your perspective, never make an emotional business decision. Stick to the facts.

Going by the numbers is really very simple. You start with the asking price. Then you work backward by listing every expense that can and will be incurred in the deal by both parties. You look for common ground. Where can you compromise on behalf of the seller without the cost to your profit margin? This is the reason why dealing with agents can be a waste of time. They simply are not interested in negotiating reality. They want to deal in potential retail market value, and you need to deal in the wholesale value.

The best way to explain and demonstrate negotiating down a price is to use a case study. The best example to demonstrate numbers is a *preforeclosure*, meaning the owner is in financial distress. It is important to understand that you need to provide a solution in the mind of the seller. You need to know what all the financial issues are. You will be appealing to his or her emotional response with what you perceive to be a logical position. Be very aware of the fact that people make emotional decisions. I'm restating that fact because it is important. How you handle a negotiation will, in the long run, define you and your credibility. You must create a report with the seller and establish credibility, or you will never be able to make a deal.

Example

The property is a single-family home. Average comparable market pricing is $400,000 based on as-is condition.

The owner has suffered a job loss and is constantly late on mortgage payments and behind two months.

The numbers are as follows:

Current Market Value	$400,000
Mortgage balance	$300,000
Mortgage penalty	$4,350
Renovations needed	$40,000

Delinquent Payments

Mortgage	$2,850
Property taxes	$1,000
Other debt—credit cards	$1,300

Legal Fees

Potential bankruptcy	$2,400
Potential foreclosure	$7,500

Marketing Costs

Realty fees (discounted to 5 percent)	$22,800
Market discount (5 percent)	$20,000

Equity

Total actual costs	$402,200
Actual	($2,200)

The Solution

The key to this example was to show the seller that he or she has no real potential for equity. Keep in mind that many deals can have equity showing on behalf of the seller. The point is to show how the price can be negotiated down with realistic cost expectations that the seller will encounter.

First off, you want the seller to get some cash out of the deal. Solve his or her problem. As a rule, you do not want to leave the seller in the property. He or she is at risk financially, and you don't want this burden. So, to start, find him or her a new home—a rental he or she can afford.

Second, negotiate with the lender to reduce or eliminate the penalties or make the existing mortgage assumable.

Third, resolve the late payments for the property taxes and personal credit.

Fourth—and this is very important—the seller isn't aware that you researched the true value of the property and found that it is not at its *highest and best use.* Many properties may have been redeveloped in the neighborhood.

This is important to recognize because you don't want to be a pioneer, meaning don't be the first to renovate and set a new market price trend in the area. You want there to be a long-term trend of properties changing use, size, type, value, and so on—for example, the structure going from a one-thousand-square-foot bungalow to a two-thousand-square-foot executive home. So, in this case, let's assume that the redeveloped market price or after-repair value (ARV) is $800,000.

Now let's look at the numbers again:

Assume the mortgage	$300,000
Cash back to the seller	$10,000
Legal fees, disbursements	$3,000
Pay off the seller's debt	$5,150
Redevelopment costs	$100,000
Reduced realtor fee of 4 percent	$30,400
Mortgages, utilities, insurance	$30,000
Subtotal	*$478,550*

Projected Sale Price

ARV less 5% for quick sale	$760,000
Projected profit:	$281,450
Cash invested:	$118,150
ROI	238%

The result of good negotiation in this case is that you resolved the seller's debt problem and helped him or her relocate. You put $10,000 cash in his or her pocket when everything to him or her seemed hopeless. The seller feels like he or she won! And you got a spectacular deal at sixty cents on the dollar, making a resounding return on investment.

This is a demonstration of how you can negotiate numbers up or down in any type of real estate or even business deal, whether it's a rehab and flip, rehab and hold, buy and hold, a wholesale, or a lease option. In the example I just gave, if you didn't have the cash to invest but wrote an offer for the deal, you could wholesale it to another investor for a fee. You can learn to use any of these strategies when investing in real estate. Be creative, but remember that in today's real estate market, the most important rule isn't just about location, location, location. It's about strategy, strategy, strategy. Knowing which one to use with an investment comes with training and experience.

Buying a property to flip, so widely shown on TV, is not as simple as they make it look. This is commonly known as the rehab-

and-flip strategy. I have learned that before you even venture into a flip, you need to be prepared. The first rule to follow in any deal is to be prepared financially. You need to have the capital or have a partner who has the capital to finance the project. Projects are easy to find; the money isn't. If you go looking, the most common question asked is "Do you have any skin in the game?" How much are you bringing to the table? One of my first attempts at a flip was a single-family home in a nice residential area. It had half-acre lots with plenty of homes already renovated. I wasn't the first. This is key because if you're the first, you may end up having a great property sitting on the market for way too long, eating your profits. Don't be a pioneer! The mistakes rehabbers often make is doing too much, not having enough money, and taking too long. You need to understand what the market in the area is demanding. The challenge in older neighborhoods is that the existing owners think their property value is at the top of the market. Even if the property is forty years old and needs a new roof, a new kitchen, a new bathroom, new windows, a new furnace, and electrical work—and we haven't even looked at the outside. Does it even have any curb appeal? But they assume that if the houses around them are selling at full market value, then they can too!

Getting back to my story, my agent turned me on to this house that was a small bungalow, a three bedroom, nothing fancy. But it was surrounded by homes twice its size, and several were renovated. The average sale prices were double what the seller was asking. Wow, a realistic home owner! I bought the property with the intention of enlarging by building an addition and installing a new kitchen and bathroom, flooring, and so on—a full renovation. I bought it for $107,000. But I didn't have the capital to renovate. I wasn't prepared. My lawyer, fortunately, did know some investors. The cost of the renovation was about $50,000, and I felt I could sell the property for over $200,000. My lawyer was also connected to one of the top real estate agents in the city at that time. We met with him to qualify what I had already determined—that I could sell for well over $200,000. All well and good until I had a look at the paperwork and the deal my lawyer set up. As it was my first flip, I hadn't realized the perceived risk an investor would account for. A hard money loan wasn't an issue for me so much as they wanted to have total control of the deal as well. If I wanted to get the project financed, I had to essentially put it in their name. If it took too long, I had to walk away. This wasn't what I wanted. I ended up walking away from that finance deal. I rented the property for a year and then sold the property as it was to only break even. Today, because I have more experience, I would have done the finance deal. We often fear the unknown. Don't let fear stand in your way. It was a great deal.

As a rehabber, you need to understand how to renovate for profit. Another caveat as an investor is you always need to have an exit strategy before you invest. This is my second most important rule.

I have owned a construction business for over thirty years, but I would never renovate based on retail construction costs. The bottom line in flipping is low cost on everything without jeopardizing quality. You need to squeeze as much value out of a dollar as you can. Piecework the labor, and buy supplies at the lowest cost possible. Find out where contractors shop for their materials. Get multiple estimates. The key to your success will be finding a reliable, cheap, experienced handyman who knows what he or she is doing. Get contractors to estimate your renovations before you make an offer on a property. Some properties only need what's called *lipstick*, essentially paint and carpet. You get in and get out as quick as possible. The more work required, the longer the flip will take. Some projects will require plans, building permits, and inspections. That process can take anywhere from a few weeks to months or even years, depending on the application. Most flips require construction time not to exceed a few months or less. If the project time requires a long period, be sure to take the holding costs into account for the entire period. The ideal flip is less than six months from purchase to renovations to marketing and finally closing the sale—basically, the shortest time possible. Time literally costs money.

It's a good idea to use an agent to sell the property and advisable to sell it just under the appraised market value by about 5 percent. The goal is to make money, not be greedy. If you wait to get *your* price, you may end up losing your profit. If you decide to sell it on your own, you better have a buyer waiting in the wings. A typical rehab property will be bought at fifty to sixty cents on the dollar based on the ARV (the after-renovation value).

You need to understand the difference between a buyer's market and a seller's market. The difference is based on supply and demand. A surplus of housing inventory could mean it's a buyer's market. A shortage would indicate that it's a seller's market. A seller's market usually will translate to quick sales and a significant increase in pricing. In a buyer's market, you will see a decrease in pricing or stagnation. Properties will take months and even, in some cases, years to sell. The sale price of a property will be directly influenced by this dynamic. In any case, the numbers need to work. Get confirmed sale prices of renovated properties similar in scope and type within a few blocks of the property.

Before you even look for property, you should have a potential list of buyers. This can be done by advertising properties for sale, for example, "We sell renovated houses below market value." Create a list of potential buyers you can call when you have a project going. Be creative with your marketing. You want to attract potential buyers to you even if you don't have a flip ready. If you know enough about social media, use the Internet to attract a buyers list. You need to be prepared. That's what savvy real estate agents do. They create lists of buyers and use the MLS system to sell them property. You can do this too. It takes work, consistent effort, and time.

The following is the accounting projection of what the numbers looked like based on the deal I discussed earlier. Keep in mind every deal is a little different, but fundamentally, you want to follow a similar strategy.

Be creative. Financing and capital can come from many sources, including mortgage brokers and private lenders, and can be traditional mortgages or hard money loans; joint venture partners or shareholders in a company you form for the deal; a blanket mortgage or equity from another property; or a line of credit. Even your lawyer can be a great source for private lenders. Using the right type of contract is important as well.

Bungalow Renovation Project

The Purchase

ARV	$240,000.00
Down payment	$17,000.00
Mortgage	$90,000.00
Closing Costs	$2,500.00
Total Purchase Cost	$109,500.00

Financing

Cash	$19,500.00
Mortgage	$90,000.00
Hard money loan	$49,680.00
Total financing cost	$159,180.00
	$20,000.00

Renovation Budget

Holding costs	$7,500.00
Hard money loan cost	$8,500.00
Marketing costs	$13,680.00
Total rehab cost	$49,680.00

The Profit Margin

Projected sale price	228,000.00
Project cost	159,180.00
Pretax profit	68,820.00

ROI	385%

The rehab and hold strategy is sometimes referred to as the "long flip." Many of these are owner occupied, mainly because they bought the property with the intention of renovating and selling but ended up living there for a few extra years—because they were unprepared. That was how one of my investment deals ended up. There's nothing wrong with holding on for some equity appreciation, but keep in mind the best real estate deals are those in which you make money when you buy, when you hold, and when you sell. If you're living in it, you can't really make money unless you're in a duplex, triplex, or fourplex. You can live in a multiunit, but be aware that it is tough to be a landlord. It's even tougher if you're living in the building. You should always consider hiring property managers or starting a property management business and having employees manage the properties.

You should be an investor first and stay an investor. Creating an independent business with residual income is about exactly that—being independent. Hire people to do the work. There are plenty of people who need jobs. Your goal should be to eventually get out of your day job and own an independent business, as soon as you can replace the income. Then you can think about retirement.

As for my long flip, here is how I did it. I bought a single-family home (SFH) $20,000 below market for $200,000. A year earlier, I got a $15,000 unsecured line of credit to invest in my RRSP. After one year, I had accumulated $20,000 and withdrew $16,000 using a registered home owner plan through my RRSP. (Keep in mind that any funds withdrawn using an RRSP home owner plan must be repaid at $1000 per year or you pay tax on the $1000 each year until the plan is fully paid off.) Then I got a 95 percent CMHC guaranteed first mortgage of $190,000 plus the insurance fee rolled in bringing the mortgage to $196,000. Closing costs were approximately $3,200. Two years into the deal, I refinanced the property at renewal with a $240,000 mortgage with a five-year term at 5 percent variable rate interest. Timing couldn't have been more perfect as the variable interest rate fell to 1.75 percent, allowing $1,000 of my $1,344 mortgage to be applied to principal. That extra principal payment allowed me to pay down my mortgage back to a balance of $200,000 in less than five years. I pulled $40,800 out tax free when I refinanced. In year seven, I refinanced the mortgage at $200,000, lowering my payment back down to $1,000 a month. I started to do the major renovations—an addition and new windows, bathrooms, kitchen, flooring, interior doors and hardware, paint, and landscaping. Renovations cost $30,000. In year ten, I sold for $328,000. For a tidy profit of $124,000 tax free after paying off the mortgage balance of $196,000 and other closing costs.

Typical rehabs require that the property be purchased at a significant discount for the numbers to work. The rehab budget needs to be within 15 to 20 percent of the ARV. What other reasons could there be for holding on to a property? The market might be a buyer's market, and the projected length of time to sell may be longer. Rather than risk leaving the property vacant, you decide to hold the property and rent it out for two years. You should always have an exit strategy on any deal. With this scenario, if it is a single-family home, you will want to make a positive cash flow. You can manage the property with a lease option that raises your initial cash profits. This can also guarantee your eventual sale price. Refinancing the property gives you extra capital to cover any negative cash flow as well. You may want to hold the property for five or ten years, looking to possibly double your equity. If the average property increase is 5 percent a year, based on the rule of 72, a property will double in value every fourteen years. If you plan to cash out by refinancing, as I did, it is tax free. Borrowed money cannot be taxed as income. As well, in Canada, the interest on any of the financing is a tax-deductible expense, provided the property is not your personal residence. In the United States, mortgage interest is deductible against personable income even if it is your primary residence.

Any money you borrow for investment or business purposes allows for the interest to be tax deductible. Depreciation on the property can also be deducted from the income, based on a forty-year amortization. In Canada, this is considered to be when you sell the property and have a capital gain. HST is only applicable on new real estate and does not apply to renovated properties. However, check with your accountant as there may be situations where the government can perceive your real estate flipping as a business in itself, and HST may apply. Everyone should try doing a flip at least once. But the big money is in holding the property for a long period. If the property is also your principal residence for at least an eight-month period, the proceeds from a sale are tax free. Any period that the property is or becomes a rental, the portion of time is prorated and taxable as a capital gain.

All the operating costs and holding costs are tax deductible. Capital expenses, such as the rehab expense itself, can be amortized or deducted from the capital gain when the property is sold. Contact an accountant to verify how these types of deductions can be applied where you live. Expenses that are classed as "chattels" can be deducted as "maintenance" expenses. An example of chattel expenses are removable fixtures, such as flooring, cabinetry, plumbing fixtures, lighting fixtures, fridges, stoves, dishwashers, microwaves, and kitchen exhaust fans. Other items that can be deducted as operating expenses are general maintenance, like painting, window cleaning, furnace repairs and cleaning, snow removal, and lawn and garden maintenance. Whenever possible, you want the tenants to pay for all utilities and provide their own insurance with a $2,000,000 liability. You will also carry insurance on the building plus liability insurance.

When I wrote the Real Business Investor Software program, I created a section called the Purchase Planner that has detailed analysis capability. I also created the Income Calculator and the Construction Calculator, which can help you calculate most expenses. These are great tools that will help you develop the strategies and analyze these investments.

The rehab-and-hold strategy can be used on any type of property—single family, multifamily, commercial, and so on. I had multiple offers, ranging from $340,000 to $350,000, but the buyers didn't qualify for financing. In the end, I sold at $328,000. About 7 percent below the fair market value based on what other properties were generally selling for during a buyer's market. If I had rented the property out, I would have made an additional $19,116 in profit, which works out to $159.30 a month in positive cash flow. But the capital gain would also have become taxable if it was a rental property. Keep in mind that I did this deal with none of my own money! I used OPM and creative financing to achieve a tax-free profit.

The following is what my long flip looked like. I bought this property during a buyer's market, and I also sold it during a buyer's market.

The Purchase

FMV	$220,000.00
Down payment	$10,000.00
Mortgage	$190,000.00
Closing costs	$3,275.00
Total purchase cost	$203,275.00

Financing

Cash	$0.00
Mortgage	$196,000.00
RRSP home-owner plan	$16,000.00
Total financing cost	$212,000.00
Tax-free cash at the buy	*$8,725.00*

Rehab and Project Costs

Renovation budget	$30,000.00
Holding costs	$0.00
Closing costs	$1,500.00
Marketing costs	$18,680.00
Total rehab cost	$50,180.00

Refinance

New mortgage	$240,000.00
Old mortgage payout	$198,000.00
Additional CMHC fee	$1,200.00
Tax-free cash out	$40,800.00

The Sale

Sale price (ARV)	$328,000.00
Total project cost	$253,455.00
Capital gain (profit)	$74,545.00

My Profit Margin

Cash out—buy	$8,725.00
Cash out—hold	$40,800.00
Cash out—sale	$74,545.00
Total tax-free profit	*124,070.00*
ROI	Infinite
Cash on cash	N/A

The buy-and-hold strategy is the best for creating long-term residual income and generational wealth. The key is to always have an exit strategy. How long do you plan to hold the property, and how are you going to sell it? Creative financing is required! A good deal is when you can make money when you buy, hold, and sell. It is a difficult strategy to do if you have no money of your own. Most lenders want to see skin in the game. Hard money is an expensive solution and should only ever be used short term.

Better solutions are private lenders that you find on your own or joint ventures with a partner. Institutional lenders, such as major banks, will usually only lend to you on three properties if your track record is pristine. The easiest private lender to find is the current owner of the property. It's called a vender-take-back (VTB) mortgage, also known as seller financing. You can also try to negotiate an agreement for deed or land contract.

A VTB is how I bought my first apartment building, a twelve unit that was a great deal. The owner wanted to retire. He was tired of being a landlord. But he still wanted an income, and he wanted to defer his capital gains tax. I made an offer to have him hold a first mortgage of $122,500, and I would give him a $500 deposit and $49,500 balance on closing. He accepted the offer with no credit check, no extra fees, and no appraisal. I came up with the $50,000 I needed plus the closing costs by borrowing against equity I had in another property. This was at a time when interest rates were double digit. The VTB was at 12 percent with a twenty-five-year amortization and no term specified and no penalty to pay off early. The equity mortgage was also at 12 percent over twenty-five years and a five-year term with a three-month penalty if I decided to pay it off early. The property was earning approximately $41,000 a year with expenses of $16,000 before debt servicing. It was a cash cow, as they say.

I tell you this story because of the mistake I made early in my career. I sold the property almost two years later for $215,000, and I made a nice profit. The mistake I made was taking advice from someone who just didn't know what he was talking about—a family member with good intentions but no business experience whatsoever. You need to find a mentor who knows what he or she is doing to avoid costly mistakes.

In fact, when I look back at the deal I made, I see that even the purchase strategy was completely by accident. I bought a cash cow with the perfect private lender. I have my agent at the time to thank for that. Rita Stortini, what a pistol. She was in her sixties at the time and had a wealth of knowledge I needed. We spent over a year looking for that property. We tried to buy a few others before we found that one. She taught me about the perfect lender and how to do it. I was only twenty-six years old at the time. She had faith in me when no one else did.

The mistake I made was selling this property at all. I had no exit strategy. What I needed to do was keep the building and pay it off. Today that building is worth approximately $1,200,000 and has a net operating income of $100,000 before any debt-financing costs. Leaving that building debt free, I could be living off that one building alone and be doing better than 95 percent of the population at retirement. In time, I could have leveraged this building and bought more income-producing property. Imagine having two of these buildings, or three. You would have a net worth over $1,000,000 and an affluent income. You would be an independent business owner with a residual-based income. I don't make these mistakes today. I hope you don't either.

Multifamily and commercial properties are the perfect buy-and-hold investments. They are bought and financed on their own ability to generate income. Any property with five or more units is considered a commercial enterprise. You may still have to provide a personal guarantee on the financing, but eventually, it won't matter. Use the right business structure. Own the properties as numbered companies that are held by a holding company. All the profits can be transferred to the holding company tax free. Only the holding company will pay tax on profits. This avoids double taxation but also gives you great asset protection. If the business income stays below $5,000,000 as a Canadian controlled corporation, you will only pay 25 percent tax on profits.

Here are the numbers on my first apartment building. You will notice the closing costs to buy are higher than the closing costs to sell. The buyer pays the land transfer tax; the seller doesn't. Land transfer tax in Ontario is 1 percent of the purchase price plus $275, although they are currently trying to change that fee structure.

The Purchase

FMV	$181,286.00
Down payment	$50,000.00
Mortgage	$122,500.00
Closing costs	$3,500.00
Total purchase cost	$176,000.00

Financing

Cash	$500.00
First mortgage	$122,500.00
Equity mortgage (another property)	$80,000.00
Total financing cost	$203,000.00

Tax-free cash out at the buy   *$27,000.00*

The Hold

Total income for the period	$65,000.00
Total expenses for the period	$48,000.00
Net income	*$17,000.00*

Refinance

FMV, based on appraisal	$200,000.00
New mortgage	$144,000.00
Mortgage payout	$122,000.00
Additional fees	$1,200.00
Tax-free cash out at refi	*$20,800.00*

The Sale

Sold	$215,000.00
Original purchase cost	$176,000.00
Closing costs	$1,500.00
Marketing costs	$12,900.00
Capital gain	*$24,600.00*

My Profit Margin

Taxable capital gain	24,600.00
Net income	17,000.00
Tax-free cash out	47,800.00
Profit	89,400.00
ROI	Infinite

In 1987, when I sold the property, the profit I made was a lot of money, especially when all of it ended up being nontaxable. The net income from the building was reduced to zero because of depreciation. The capital gain of $24,600 and recaptured depreciation were tax exempt because of a lifetime $100,000 exemption allowable at the time. Plus, the tax-free mortgage cash outs totaled $20,300. My net profit on this deal was over $62,400 plus the tax-free cash out from the equity mortgage of $27,000, from another property used to facilitate this deal, for a total of $89,400 in an eighteen-month period from real estate alone. In today's dollars, that would be approximately $180,000. Sounds great, but I should have kept this one. This property would be providing a net annual income after expenses of more than $100,000 a year and be worth over $1,200,000. Over thirty years, this property easily would have produced well over $1,000,000 in net accumulated income alone, not including the million plus net worth in equity. Imagine if you owned five of these, buying just one every five years. You could have a net income, after tax, of more than $250,000 a year and a net worth more than $5,000,000. That is generational wealth!

A *wholesale assignment* is when you contract a property "in trust" with the sole purpose of selling the contract to another buyer or investor. You may not have the money to invest. You do, however, have control of a property with an "offer to purchase." You can sell the contract to someone who can buy. As with any property, your intention is to get the property at a discounted price based on a problem. Properties with problems can include not but are not limited to preforeclosures, rehabs, estate sales, divorce, abandonment, and vacant FSBOs. Wholesaling real estate, as some refer to this strategy, is in fact the process of selling your contract by assigning it to another buyer.

You will need your own lawyer to act on your behalf with this type of deal. In fact, always use your own lawyer to avoid conflict-of-interest issues. The original seller and your buyer need to have their own lawyers. The seller does not need to know about the assignment. The negotiations for the assignment are with your buyer. You should have a list of investor buyers in advance to sell these contracts to, such as contractors, renovators, and seasoned investors. There is no limit on the amount of discount you want to negotiate with the seller except that your buyer/investor needs to see the potential profit. Research is key to understanding the true value of a deal. Often, assignments fees are low, in the $1,000 range.

I have attended many real estate investment courses where they promote the concept of writing as many offers as possible, hoping you get one that sticks. This is a hit-and-miss strategy and not one that any realtor will want to do for you. If you try the multiple-offer technique, use it with FSBOs. I tend to believe that you should spend time finding a deal that is a deal, not throwing mud on the wall hoping some will stick. Find a deal. Let time compound your investment. Create wealth.

Over the years, I have had the opportunity to use this strategy on a few occasions. The first time I was approached was on a deal that kind of fell into my lap and then fell right back out. I was looking at a property with a young realtor. The property I was looking at, at the time, didn't fit my plan, so he indicated to me that there was a new listing in his office that was literally less than twenty-four hours old—a three-row town-house building. The owner was desperate, as she was losing money. So I wanted to take a peek.

The building was vacant, I found out it had legal severance on all three units, and the owner had a recent appraisal of $240,000. The existing first mortgage was $175,000 and assumable. I made an offer of $175,000 with a few escape clauses, such as conditional on financing and a clause allowing a two-week period to have the building inspected. I threw a low-ball offer. I wanted to see how desperate the seller was. I was shocked she accepted it. I set out preparing a proposal for an investor I knew who had looked at other deals with me. Unfortunately, he was out of town for the two weeks. Timing was lousy. Unknown to me, at the same time, my newbie realtor was bragging in the office of the quick sale. A senior realtor who was also an investor heard what was going on. My strategy, after conferring with my lawyer, was to just assume the mortgage and close. We could deal with the redevelopment of the property after.

The senior realtor realized what I was doing, went behind my back, and negotiated a backup offer with the seller for $180,000. Then he called the lender who owned the mortgage, an insurance company, and notified them of the pending sale. This triggered a due-on-sale clause. Even though the mortgage was assumable, they wanted the right to approve the borrower. That would be me. I didn't have the income at the time, and I knew I wouldn't get approved. This was a backhanded strategy by the realtor/investor. The next day, I got a call from a lawyer I had dealt with on another property deal. He asked if I wanted to sell my offer for $1,000. I had never heard of this before. It turned out he was also the investor-realtor's lawyer. I put two and two together. In fact, this lawyer was someone I knew who had handled a mortgage deal for me two years earlier.

My lawyer knew very little about assignments at the time but was now thinking that something was not quite right, that I might be putting myself at risk. He counseled me, and I decided to waive my condition and let the deal go. The other investor wanted my deal because it would have saved him $4,000; plus, I opened the door to a deal that was $65,000 below market and 70 percent of the as-is appraised value. The ARV was at least $100,000 per unit severed at a minimum, making its purchase value at less than 60 cents on the dollar. Its highest and best use would have been a twelve-unit redevelopment worth $720,000 at the time, making its purchase value essentially for land value, which was what I was looking at. Obviously, it was a spectacular deal. In the end, he gave up his real estate license, I believe for violating conflict-of-interest rules. But he got his property. He felt guilty enough that he bought my research on the property for $1,000 and then hired me as a contractor on the project. He kept it as a three-unit. I don't believe he sold it off. He kept it as a rental property. I think he was worried about being sued. Luckily for him, I was not the litigation type of guy others would be. That was my first potential assignment deal. But I still made some money.

Later in my investing career, I did have the opportunity to structure a real assignment deal. I placed an offer, in trust, on a four-plex that was also another vacant renovation project. This time, I had an investor prepared to buy. The property closed. I made a $6,000 net assignment fee. I also invested in a mortgage on the property; I charged points and a setup fee, earning me another $2,500 plus 10 percent interest per annum on the hard money mortgage.

Generally, most assignments are in the $1,000 range. The deals need to be profitable to the investor/buyer you sell to. You can make money from real estate without actually owning it. The key is the contract. The offer to purchase is in fact a contract. Once you have a seller who accepts and signs the offer, you take control of the property. It can't be sold or conveyed to anyone else as long as you have a signed contract. To fulfill the obligations of the contract, all the clauses must be met. You always put clauses in the contract that allow you time to fulfill them—conditions such as financing, inspection, lawyer's approval, and so on. You must also make the contract out to either your name or a company name, "in trust." This allows your lawyer to legally transfer the property at the closing date to whomever you appoint because now it has become a "trust deal."

The process is a two-part transaction. The first part is called an "assignment." The second part is the "wholesale" portion of the real estate deal. You're buying a property at a discount and wholesaling it to another buyer. The following chart shows the numbers on the assignment I mentioned earlier. This was a four-plex renovation deal bought for land value and flipped (wholesaled) to another investor. I also gave him a hard money mortgage I set up out of my personal (self-directed) RRSP as a third-party arm's-length mortgage transaction, where I acted as the bank. It was a very sophisticated deal that I had to teach my lawyer how to do.

The Purchase

FMV	$50,000
Down payment	$500
Cash	$47,000
Closing costs	$3,500
Total	*$51,000*

The Assignment

Legal fees	$1,500
Assignment fee	$6,000
Total	*$7,500*

Projected Financing and Costs

Investor / cash	$79,700
Hard money mortgage	$86,000
Points and fees	$2,500
Total	*$175,000*

The Wholesale

Property value (ARV)	$222,000
Purchase costs	$58,500
Construction costs	$96,500
Closing costs	$3,500
Interest costs	$17,200
Total	*$175,000*

The Investor

Potential profit	$46,300
Two-year ROI	42.6%

My Profit Margin

Assignment fee	$6,000
Points and fees	$2,500
Interest	$17,200
Total	*$25,700*

Investment	$86,000
ROI	30%
Annualized ROI	15%

The lease option strategy is also a great way to control real estate without actually owning it. Lease options are a challenge to accomplish, as rental agreements typically cost the potential buyers more money than a standard lease agreement. All contracts have value, whether you invest money or not. You can make a profit with them. The key with this strategy is to find buyers who have money but damaged credit. They have steady income, can afford to pay an inflated rent, and have a cash down payment. Tenants who have the perception of ownership tend to pay their rent on time. They realize that if they break their lease, they may lose all or a portion of their deposit. And they will take care of and maintain the property at their expense. Note that when you contract with tenants in this manner and they break the lease, they may expect some or all of their accumulated down payment returned. Be sure to have your lawyer draft an iron-clad rental agreement and that the buyers are clear in their understanding of the nonrefundable deposit. The key is to not be greedy. You're making free money on these deals. To find rent-to-own buyers, just place an ad. They will contact you.

If the buyer has, for example, $20,000 for a deposit. Only take 50 percent and have them use the balance to cover the increase in rent that can be accumulated toward their deposit. Have them put the difference in a term deposit to be used for them to buy the home at the end of the lease option. Counsel them. Remember, you are helping them to repair their credit and buy a home. You will want to know what their debts are. Get them to sign a release allowing you to contact their creditors. They need to have full disclosure with you. Have them fill out a rental application allowing you to do a credit check. The buyer must be able to save money for the closing costs and can be preapproved for a 90 percent mortgage by the end to the lease term.

There are two basic strategies: the sandwich lease option and a standard lease option. A lease option is when you use a rental lease agreement combined with an option to purchase the property with specific terms and conditions. The option comes with a nonrefundable deposit. The term of the rental lease is typically twelve to twenty-four months. The purchase price of the property is set at a predetermined price, usually by the average inflation rate of property in the area. This is published by real estate boards across the country. The lease payment is negotiated. Typical lease option rental costs are calculated by the seller's mortgage payment plus insurance costs plus property taxes and a small cash flow profit. The rental payment can also include a refundable deposit amount negotiated with the buyer. If he or she terminates the lease or doesn't exercise his or option to buy at the end of the lease, he or she is entitled to a refund of the accumulated deposit without interest—not the nonrefundable deposit.

A good practice if no accumulative purchase deposit is part of the deal is to give the buyer a credit portion from his or her rental agreement. The buyer is also responsible for all utilities and maintenance. As a future home owner, buyers usually have no issues with this. Any major repairs will be at the owner's expense. The sandwich lease option comes into play when you in turn sublease the property to another buyer following the same lease option formulae but add more inflation to the sale price. Be realistic. The idea is to make money not get rich off one deal. Typical inflation rates are 5 percent a year.

Two rental agreements and options are involved: option 1 between you (Buyer A) and the seller and option 2 between you and your buyer (Buyer B). The sandwich lease allows you to make money when you buy from the differential in nonrefundable deposits. Earning rental income from (the "hold") is based on the differential between the two rental agreements. You also make a profit (the sale) based on the differential between the two offer-to-purchase agreements that are part of the option that gets exercised at the end of the lease option term. Closing costs include land transfer fees and title insurance and legal fees. A great strategy to manage SFH vacancies is to use a lease option (option 1 only) with a nonrefundable deposit. The deposit covers any foreseeable negative cash flow, and you get a tenant who maintains the property for you at their expense.

Lease Option 1

FMV of property, year one	$100,000.00
Option purchase price	$99,000.00
Nonrefundable deposit	$5,000.00
Rental agreement, monthly	$1,000.00
Monthly deposit amount	$100.00

Legal fees, if applicable	$495.00
Accumulative deposit	$2,400.00
Inflation rate	5%
Equity	$10,000.00
Term	24 months

Exercise the Option

Double closing with option 2	
Balance owed the seller at closing	$82,600.00

Lease Option 2

FMV of property in two years	$108,900.00
Option purchase price	$108,900.00
Nonrefundable deposit	$10,000.00
Rental agreement, monthly	$1,100.00
Monthly deposit amount	$100.00
Legal fees, if applicable	$544.50
Accumulative deposit	$2,400.00
Inflation rate	5%
Equity	$20,250.00
Term	24 months

Exercise the Option

Mortgage qualification	$100,950.00
High ratio insurance fee (CMHC), included above	$2,940.30
Closing costs	$2,803.00
Balance owed at closing	$10,890.00
Total deposit applied	$12,400.00
Cash required by Buyer B	$1,293.00

The Profit Margin

Nonrefundable deposit	Buy	$5,000.00
Rental income	Hold	$2,400.00
Sales profit	Sell	$12,905.00
Total profit		$20,305.00

Break the common mold of get a good education,

get a good job with a pension mentality!

—Gregory M. Luchak

Secret Video #7

www.TheWealthPrinciple.net/chapter_seven.html

Chapter 7

The Perfect Business

The meaning of life is to find your gift.
The purpose of life is to give it away.
—Pablo Picasso

Have you ever thought that someday you want to become your own boss? To own your own business? That you would like to invest? Own real estate? Own multiple businesses? Have a residual-based income and leave a financial legacy for your family? But how?

Is there such a thing as the perfect business? Absolutely! Most businesses can be described as conventional. They start out with a plan and some capital to develop the opportunity. Almost all businesses need employees, a place of business, tools, equipment, inventory, insurance, and some working capital just to get started. They also require some form of business registration, government accounts, and regulatory filings. They also require a lot of capital to grow to become self-sufficient. For those who don't quite understand what capital is, it's *cash* to grow the business.

Then there are unconventional businesses, the type that need really none of the above. Very little cash is required. They can be developed with limited time and effort compared to a conventional business or a job. Imagine a business you can develop that could run on autopilot. Every month, you get paid whether you are present or not. Could this really be true? Or does it sound too good to be true? The fact is they do exist. Everybody wants to have a residual-based income, to get paid with very little effort. The fact is anyone could be in business without the risk if he or she knew how. But I will tell you that in the beginning, it will take tremendous effort. As your business grows, that effort can be reduced.

131

Before I get into this next session, I want to tell you about a personal experience. I attend a lot of seminars. Some might say that I am a seminar junkie. I believe in knowledge, and the knowledge I look for isn't taught in school. Specifically, I am always in search of entrepreneurial knowledge and personal development.

So I attended a boot camp on, of all things, how to write and publish a book. Since I had never published a book, I wanted to learn how I could and make money. It was important to me.

The speaker was insightful, and the course was very informational. The mentor who owned this training company, in fact, is a well-known and highly successful author of many books. I learned a lot by attending the boot camp. Overall, I was satisfied with the speaker who was teaching. However, during one of the sessions, the speaker thought it was important to tell a story that the mentor of this boot camp had relayed to him. The part that got under my skin a little was that he thought it would be appropriate to make what I felt was disparaging comments toward a company he made obvious to me that he knew nothing about.

The mentor's story goes as follows. He had become a successful author and was somewhat well known at a time. Early in his career, a former classmate of his called him up after about eight years and invited him and his wife to dinner at his home to catch up on old and new times. He agreed. And they attended. Everything went well until another guest got up between dinner and dessert and pulled up a flip chart. He started to do a presentation. I won't identify the company, but it was at this point in the speaker's story that he said, "Yep, another (bleep bleep) home meeting." He described how angry his mentor was that he was invited to this dinner under false pretense. He implied by his body language and comments that it was the company and not the people giving the presentation at fault, essentially implying or, I would say, inferring that the company was well known for not being a good company.

Now, as you can well imagine, he was referring to a company that I was affiliated with. I didn't say anything, but I did think to myself, Here is yet another person passing himself off as an expert in a field he knows little about.

The speaker began the boot camp by talking about how he was once upon a time doing well in a multilevel. He had sponsored over six hundred people. A few years into it, the multilevel shut down. He got discouraged. Being that he developed an Multi Level Marketing (MLM) business, he believed he was an expert.

First, the principles that you learn in how to market and build a business like an MLM are universal. So, he could have gone to literally any other MLM and had success—being that he could successfully sponsor people, or so he thought. Second, if he was experienced enough, he would have known that you never invite people to any kind of event, let alone a dinner, under false pretense. You see, it wasn't the MLM company's fault; it was the fault of the people conducting the meeting and anyone who counseled them to do so.

Just as a quick coaching note—if you ever decide to participate in an MLM, you don't conduct your business in that fashion. Yes, you certainly can have home meetings, hotel meetings, and meetings in coffee shops or wherever. But anyone who knows about marketing knows that when you prospect anyone, you have a conversation and ask questions. You want to identify a problem and provide a solution.

Had the person simply asked the mentor if he was looking for an opportunity, the mentor could have said yes or no. He would have known from the start what the purpose of the dinner was. I tell you this story because I am about to discuss an incredible opportunity most have heard of but few have ever been asked to check out, let alone participate in. Yet most have an expert opinion and think they know what they are talking about because they knew someone who knew someone who knew someone who had a bad experience. This is simply not accurate and the furthest thing from the truth.

I can tell you from personal experience that anyone who knows me knows that I am an entrepreneur and have always been driven to own a business. I know a lot of people. A lot of people know me. You are no different. We all have personal connections, and most people don't even realize they have. And yet in the past forty years, I have only ever been asked to look at a business opportunity twice—once by a friend who knew I was in business and once by a client who knew I was involved with a competing MLM business. When I talk to people, most even still today have never been asked to look at a business opportunity. Yet most people think about it and even secretly wish for it. But they just don't know how to get started.

How would you like to have a business that can generate all the capital you need to become an entrepreneur, an independent business owner, or even an investor? The main reason I wrote this book, which has morphed into a coaching and training program, was to help and teach people that anyone with the desire can become an entrepreneur with absolutely no experience—as long as you have the absolute desire to win!

If you have the capital to start a business, that's great, but what if you don't? What if you don't even have the credit to borrow? What if you need more than just a book! You need structure, business tools, and training? Maybe you would like to learn from a business mentoring program. Then I suggest the perfect business may be just what you are looking for.

What is the "perfect business"? Well, simply put, it's a direct sales business using a multilevel marketing business model. Yes, an MLM! The reason I label this type of business as the perfect business is because literally anyone can start with no money and no experience and do it part time while carrying on with regular income from a job. At the same time, you can be receiving coaching and mentoring, accessing a business training program. You can invest into your business as it grows. There is no limit to the success you can have, except the limits you put on yourself.

> Opportunity is missed by most people because it is dressed in overalls and looks like work.
> —Thomas Edison

Before you decide to start a business, you should understand why this business model is so powerful and why you should consider it as a starting point and a solution to getting started in business. Open your mind up. Look at life outside of the box we all live in. This is where you will begin to learn how entrepreneurs think, act, and make the world go around.

First, let's start by understanding that we all have personal capital that we are unaware of. Every day, we spend money buying consumer goods and services at full retail. Every time you walk into a big box store, as an example, you are spending money, putting profits directly into the pockets of the owner. There's nothing wrong with that if you plan to be an employee the rest of your life.

Maybe you're not interested in financial freedom. But imagine for a moment that you are now a business owner. Does it make sense to be spending 100 percent of your (hard-earned) money buying products and services at full retail? Think about the home you bought or rent at full market value, the food you buy at the grocery store, and everything you spend money on in between. Much of people's net income is spent buying stuff. That's a lot of money. I could say they are spending 165 percent of their disposable annual income. For most people, that is an absolute fact.

The second part of this equation I like to talk about is how to turn the rest of your (hard-earned) money that you spend on what I call "stuff" into working capital the smart way. It's a lot of money. As an example, let's say the average family, based on the statistics I gave you earlier, has a typical net monthly income. They are not poor but not rich by any means, simply earning an average middle-class income. On average, a least 30 percent of their income is being spent on everyday stuff every month. A minimum of 20 percent of that money is going into someone else's pocket (a for-profit business) as profit. Could be Walmart, Loblaw's, Costco, Target...Pick one! They all profit from you every time you shop. Why not put the profit back into your pocket?

Third, you need to change the way you think about your money. You want to start treating your own money as if you were investing it into your own business!

Literally, the consumer market is a multitrillion-dollar market that you can take advantage of. Remember that in business, it's not who or what you know; It's how you think. And at this moment, it's how you are thinking that is holding you back.

Now I don't want to be giving away a proprietary business model. So, I will talk in general terms. Let's take an example of how you can turn a portion of the net income you already spend supporting someone else's business into supporting your own business. That's roughly the 20 percent minimum you're giving away to big-box stores. Now, most multilevel businesses sell consumer products and services. They base their business model on the fact that consumers buy these products and services at full retail. Why not buy at a discount? In a group setting? Many people as a group are powerful. And they know it.

You could be buying most of your personal products and services at wholesale or at a substantial discount, creating a residual-based business income in the process.

Not only will you be saving money, but you could be making money off your own spending habits. So, to start, you need to change your personal spending habits.

Next let us expand the box you're thinking out of. How many people live on your street? In your neighborhood? Your city? Think of it in terms of their spending. If the average person is spending just like you—and they may even be spending a lot more than you do—how much money is that? Let's not make it too mind boggling. If there are a thousand houses in your neighborhood, that equates to millions of dollars a month collectively they're spending at the store. In my opinion, that is a low-ball number. The actual amount of money people spend monthly is much higher than what I am talking about.

Now let's think about franchising the idea out. How many people in your neighborhood would want to save and make money simply by changing their personal spending habits! You get the idea?

You could start a revolution in your own community!

Now as an example based on today's economics, if you could help just a fraction of those families do just what you're doing, creating a business based on their personal spending habits, based on the right business structure, you could be making a significant income. That is residual, recurring income that grows as the business grows—independent of you.

The more people you help convert their expenses into profits, the more everyone can make, spending what I call "anyway money." That's money you're going to spend anyway.

Whether you get involved in a business or not, imagine how many people, how many households, are in your neighborhood, all doing just what we all do, spending money every day, every week, every month buying stuff, like gas for the car or a grande mocha latte at the coffee shop, the next hot smartphone, school supplies, building materials, clothes for the kids, or a new suit of clothes, business cards, thank-you cards, a laptop computer, and vitamins from the pharmacy or traveling to thousands of hotels and destinations around the world. Just imagine thousands of households spending thousands of dollars a month, spending money on their MasterCard and Visa, buying all kinds of products and services.

The next time you spend your (hard-earned) money on a product, ask yourself, Am I getting paid to use this product? You and your friends could be getting paid a residual income based on all that spending.

The consumer market is a multitrillion-dollar market, and you are already participating in it. Why not get something back? Why not help a few of your friends make a residual income?

Now what if your goal is to become affluent? Would you want to invest in real estate? Maybe even invest in or start other businesses?

The fact is the multilevel business model has little competition compared to a traditional business. Dollar-wise these businesses are the lowest cost for a business start-up you can participate in. As a business, the more people you help, the more everyone wins. The competition that exists is between the companies in the multi-level industry. As a company, they welcome competition because the competition provides a level of confirmation that the market exists. Now, how you pick a multilevel company depends on what your belief system is. The business principles that you learn through personal development from a multilevel platform are universal.

Many people bounce from company to company because they think this one works better than that one or that one pays better than another one. Eventually, they find out that the one they believed in didn't believe in them. They shut down the business. That happened to the speaker I mentioned earlier. Everyone thinks a new company is a ground-floor opportunity. This is not always the case. You should research and understand who the company is and who the people behind it are. What are their core values? It isn't just about the money, even though it is the money that everyone gets excited about.

The key here is that you need to learn how to build a business. A good multilevel can teach you how. So, the question becomes, how good of a student can you be? You can make money anywhere in any business when you learn and understand the principles for success and wealth creation.

All MLMs teach you how you could be making six or even seven figures simply by duplicating your efforts. If you're making $150,000 a year and living on $50,000 a year, how much real estate could you invest in? How big will your empire be?

In terms of a pension, that can be astronomical! Fantastic! If you think I'm being a little over the top, ask anyone who is on a pension what they make? How much is their old-age security? Ask a

Millennial! They will likely laugh and say, "What pension? What old-age security? It won't exist for me."

Typically, you keep your present job. Once you become successful part time, would you keep working your regular job? That is the power of using a multilevel business as an entry point into creating wealth if you don't have the cash or the know-how.

If you could be among the 3 percent of income earners, how would your lifestyle change? Where would you live? Where would you travel? How often would you travel? Wouldn't it be nice to pay cash for everything?

Welcome to the world of an independent-thinking business owner and investor.

Start thinking out of the box. Start to think big. There is a revolution happening. After every recession, there is a great boom. The great boom of this century is almost upon us, and you will be a part of it. The question is will you profit from it?

If you keep your present job, working for that pension, spending your (hard-earned) money, will you ever have enough to retire? Do you really believe that you can save your way to prosperity?

How much money would you need to have invested to generate a monthly income that matches your present income when you retire? Based on today's economics, what you would need to gross just to be a part of the middle class? How much would you need to buy a home and keep it without going broke in the process?

To earn an average middle-class income of $6,200 a month in today's dollars, you would need $7.4 million earning 1 percent interest in a bank. Or...you would need $2.9 million earning 3 percent interest in a retirement income fund. Or...you would need $1.5 million invested in real estate earning a 5 percent cash on cash return.

How much would you have to save to replace your income to retire at sixty-five years old and continue to live until you're one hundred years old?

If your desired retirement income was simply $50,000 a year, you would need to save $3,086.42 a month at an average annual interest rate of 3 percent for forty-five years to acquire $1,666,666.67. Literally you would have to start at age twenty, and that feat as an employee is never going to happen in today's economy. You could however do it by starting a business.

The perfect business is right in your own neighborhood. The households and the real estate people live in are literally a gold mine of opportunity that they could all participate in if they had the knowledge and the desire.

Now you do!

Have you heard the story of the farmer's dog? I heard this story once before, and to the best of my knowledge, the original author is unknown. I looked to find the author but couldn't. So, I will give credit to the speaker who told the story. She may even be the author. Her name is Julie Donovan. She's a very successful entrepreneur from Florida. So, I am going to paraphrase the story as I remember it.

Farmer John was sitting on his porch one rainy afternoon. His friend Bill came to visit. As Bill and John were sitting watching the storm, Farmer John's dog, Rusty, was lying beside them on the porch. As he lay there, Bill could hear the dog moan. A little time had passed, and again the dog moaned. Bill thought this was a little strange but continued to chat with Farmer John. A short time later, Bill could hear the dog moan again. So, he decided he'd better ask Farmer John.

"What is wrong with Rusty, John?"

"Oh, don't be bothered by old Rusty. He's been lying on that nail all day long and can't be bothered enough to get up and move!"

Does that story remind you of anybody?

People complain and moan every day about the situations they are in. But few do anything about them. The moral of the story is that you can get up and do something to change your circumstances, to change your life, and move on. You'll know you're on the right track when you start investing in yourself with knowledge and following someone who is going in the direction you want to go!

The wealth principle is not just an idea; it is a series of strategies and principles that create a system that you can implement into your life's daily activity.

The perfect business is the one you start and succeed at by learning, failing, getting up, and starting again and never ever quitting, because you have belief and faith in your ability to succeed, no matter what. You may not have the financial means to start a business or invest in real estate, but now you have some basic knowledge and a great idea on how to get started. Take this system to the next level, and learn how you can build a great life and an empire in the process.

Learn from failure. If you are an entrepreneur and your first venture wasn't a success, welcome to the club!
—Richard Branson

Secret Video #8

www.TheWealthPrinciple.net/chapter_eight.html

Chapter 8

How to Be an Effective Entrepreneur

Entrepreneurship is living a few years of your life
like most people won't, so that you can spend the rest of
your life like most people can't.
—Unknown

Over the past decade or so, I wrote several articles I posted on the blog page of my website. They reveal the top strategies and insights on entrepreneurship and how to reach your goals and ultimately your dreams. I drew inspiration from some of them while writing this book.

Being an effective entrepreneur relies on your ability to be humble, grateful, giving, resourceful, practical, inspired, and the leader everyone hopes you are. You also need to be an absolute sponge when it comes to knowledge.

Here are a few of my favorite articles that reveal a few more of those strategies I have written about throughout this book.[16]

---

[16] Articles have been edited for clarity and formatting.

Friday, February 3, 2012

The Perfect Storm

By Greg Luchak

Master Renovator, Contractor, and Entrepreneur

I'm sitting here in my basement with half a bottle of water; it's 1:00 a.m., and I'm wondering, How can I get your attention? Will you really listen?

Grab a cup of coffee or a bottle of water, shut the idiot box off, stop tweeting for a minute or two, and spend a few more minutes with me.

Remember the movie *Pretty Woman* with Julia Roberts? The scene where the guy is walking down the street and in the background you hear, "What's your dream?"

Ever really ask yourself what your dream really is?

Isn't it about time you did something about it?

It starts with a decision…Keep reading!

You've likely heard this statement many times before: "There is no better time than right now to get into business"—right?

I can tell you this based on thirty plus years of experience in business that that statement is very true. I believe it because I understand it. Whether you got into business last year, ten years ago, or right now, the fact is it's always a good idea and the right time to get into business.

Now some will argue that you can get into a business too late in an industry or market. That is one perspective. Another is you can get into business, and despite the timing, the money, the trends, or the product, you can learn to make it be successful in any market condition.

My point is that if you can start a business in the worst of times and be successful, just imagine how successful it will be in the best of times. Some will say that we are possibly in the worst economic times in our history since the Great Depression.

Again, it's all about perspective.

Every opportunity has a silver lining if you know where to look.

So, do you know where to look?

Let me take a little bit of the guess work out of it for you. Unless you have been under a rock in the wilderness with no TV, Internet, cell phone, land line, or billboards to look at, you have heard of Facebook and social media—a billion plus users. You've also heard about countless people losing their jobs and their homes, and you may even know a few. The wars are ending, the wars are not ending, yet another election.

Wow—everyone is freaking out over this stuff!

Let's back up a bit and look at what you and I and most of the planet have witnessed over the years. Think about our forebears, the people who immigrated to the western hemisphere looking for an opportunity they couldn't find at home. Opportunity really started to take a foothold with the Industrial Revolution—the printing press!

Now, I don't want to lose you here.

There is a point to this history lesson so keep reading and I will get to it...

It wasn't too long before the Gold Rush came along...

Then it was *oil* and in between every boom and bust opportunity were real estate booms and busts.

In the seventies, you had to know enough to pick VHS over Beta, but VCRs were the technology of the decade.

Then came the eighties with the personal computer.

How about the nineties when it became all about the Internet and dot-coms.

In the new millennium, health and wellness is the leading trend.

Business in the Western Hemisphere (or just about anywhere in the free world) is all about distribution.

Gone are the days of manufacturing and job security.

The baby boomers consistently have set the trends we have lived with for the past forty years.

Someone once said, "The procrastinators are the leaders of tomorrow." (Ha ha!)

I hope you are not one of them!

Really...

Gen-Y, Gen-X, and the Millennials are the leaders of tomorrow. But what are they going to be leading with?

The information we are all seeking is all around us literally being flaunted in our faces.

The question is can you see it for all the noise and propaganda?

And there is a lot of propaganda.

We are saturated with messages from every medium.

Beware of the fool's gold of today! It's in your face every day too!

You look at the economy today, thinking about owning a business, and are mesmerized by the speed of technology and the cool stuff we can use today—like smartphones, tablets, HD video, and social media. Our imagination is overwhelmed by the likes of Facebook, Google, YouTube, Twitter, Apple, and so on. Right?

So, you're asking, "What is the point of all this and owning a business?"

Well, begin to ask yourself the following:

What are the experts telling us all the time?

"Own your own business!"

Why are they telling us this?

Because being an employee (paid slavery) doesn't work for anyone who wants anything of any value in his or her future! This most definitely means no chance at a worthwhile pension. Do you want to be an employee for the rest of your life? Awesome. Do you want to be wealthy? You need to change your perspective.

Who is telling us?

People like Warren Buffet, Donald Trump, Richard Branson, Robert Kiyosaki, Paul Zane Pilzer, Harry S. Dent Jr., and too many others to mention right now are! Even major banks, institutions, research companies, and think tanks have released studies and surveys that state one in five people want to own a business. They also state that 87 percent of people who retire go back to work because they can't afford not to work.

The writing is on the wall all around us.

So, what kind of business should we be in?

Every one of the experts I just mentioned have all stated that the number-one type of business in the world that anyone wanting to start a business with no experience should get into is a network marketing business.

Now some may ask why.

I as well as many others would say, "Why not? And why not *you*?"

I can tell you why! And I will also tell you why right now is the best time in history. The evidence is all around us in plain sight. The number one reason you should get into business is because you want more out of life. I already stated that, but it needs to be reinforced.

Why? Because your reason. Why? Your dreams, your aspirations, and even your desperations are what fuel you to succeed even when by all odds it seems like you should fail. Never quitting, following a mentor, and using a proven training system, combined with a proven distribution system, quite frankly just works if you work it.

But getting back to why now!

I will save you the long version and tell you this:

Everything in life has its own cycle. Some call it an S curve, the highs and lows, the ebbs and flows.

The economy has a cycle.

Every country has its own cycle.

Every industry has a cycle.

Products and services have their own cycle.

Every business has a cycle.

Every team has a cycle.

Groups of people, even individual people, have a cycle.

Even you and I each have a cycle in our life of highs and lows.

Here is the cool thing.

It's what I call the perfect storm, and it is happening *right now*!

All the experts know what I'm talking about.

It's the reason why some people become wealthy and other people become poor! There are those rare times in life when most of the cycles converge and meet at their lowest point. They have nowhere else to go but up! And, no, I don't mean run out and buy bitcoins or Facebook stock. The Internet, Facebook, Twitter, Google, all the social media, and all the new technologies for most people are only tools we learn to use in business. Sure, some people will make a fortune with those technologies. But I will let you know something…they're already in position to do so—and *you are likely not*!

Don't be trapped by those who want to sell you the magic bullet. There is none. *You're it!*

There is no shortcut. A real business takes time and effort. There is a learning curve. I think you know what I'm talking about. If not, feel free to ask me.

The real training you're looking for isn't sold by some affiliate program. Don't be trapped by the fool's gold that pervades the Internet.

There has never been a better time than *right now* to own a business. It could be a network marketing business or a real estate business or some other business.

If you build it *right now*, you will catch the wave.

If you wait five years, like most people, thinking you'll get involved when the market and economy are hot again, you will miss out on the most profitable time in recent history.

It's all about positioning, and the experts know this.

They have been telling us for years. But they also know that most people's eyes are glazed over and their ears are blocked.

I will give you one example I learned from listening to Warren Buffet. What I learned from him was this:

"Know your business. Don't invest in speculation."

Opportunity is knocking. Is anyone home?

The perfect storm is here.

Remember where we started: "What's your dream?"

Decide to find out how you can get started! Today!

Friday, March 2, 2012

The Eight-Step Pattern to Success

By Greg Luchak
Master Renovator, Contractor, and Entrepreneur

Seventy million North Americans may be looking for the business opportunity of a lifetime without even knowing it! Recent reports summarizing the consumer outlook highlight that one in five are thinking of starting their own business within the next five years. North America has been suffering through the greatest recession in history since the Great Depression. Earning a living as an employee is no guarantee and proving to be getting more and more difficult. On the other side of the coin, owning a business has never been easier than it is right now!

However, those same reports say that 28 percent of potential entrepreneurs have concerns about finding start-up or expansion money. Fourteen percent also worry about finding clients, and others feel it would take too long to turn a profit. That's a few very real roadblocks preventing people from going after their dreams.

The eight-step pattern to success in life and business starts with a dream. You must have a passion and a desire to win and the resiliency to fail forward and never quit. That is the true key to success right there.

It doesn't matter how long it takes or how many mistakes you make.

You learn as an entrepreneur and in life to pick yourself up, dust yourself off, and keep going. Period!

Success has nothing to do with how fast you get there. It's not a race; it's a process! That process starts with your personal commitment to yourself—not anyone else. You will learn that you are the magic to your own success.

The eight-step pattern in any business is essential. Quite frankly, it just works. If no one has ever showed or explained this to you, then let me be the first. It doesn't matter. Remember, it's not a race. Even if it takes you thirty years to make your dreams come true, the only one who will know that it took that long likely will be you.

How many times have you heard about the guy who was an overnight success? That simply is rarely the truth. Often, that person spent months, even years practicing and learning and failing forward over and over. Then finally someone notices, and they think, Wow! How did he do that? He must have had some secret formula. Right?

In business and in life, the formulas are simple. It's not a secret; it's a pattern. You need to take some simple steps and follow through and then repeat the pattern over and over and over. Your success will come from the habits you create.

Step 1: Your Dream

Without a dream, you will never ever do anything more than what's necessary to stay right where you are. So, dream big. The bigger, the better. But remember to set goals to achieve your dream. Otherwise, it's just a pipe dream. And all you will end up being is just another dreamer.

Setting goals will make dreams come true.

Step 2: Your Commitment

You must have focused effort. You need to make decisions even if sometimes your decisions are wrong. You will learn from those decisions because you made a commitment to never give up. You made a commitment to your dream.

Step 3: Make a List

Write down your dreams, your goals, and the people you want to include. People are the missing ingredient; most are either afraid to include or approach them. No business on earth exists or succeeds without people. You need to create a power team to work with you.

You need people to present your idea, your product, or your service too! You need to prioritize and categorize your list.

Step 4: The Invitation

Simply put, you need to learn how to ask people. Ask for help. Ask people if they are interested in what you're doing. Find a coach, a mentor, and ask for help. The invitation doesn't end there. You also need to learn how to invite, to qualify the people you are inviting. Learn to interview and ask questions. You're looking for people who can help you.

More important, find people you can help in the process. Some might call it "paying it forward." People will be more willing to join you if they believe you are helping them.

Step 5: Share Your Plan

Start the process of reaching your goals by sharing your plans, your business ideas. And here is a reality check. It doesn't even have to be your idea or your business plan. Find a business model and a mentor who can help you succeed with your plan. Use the credibility of your mentor and your power team. Reinventing the wheel is hard to do. Get help. Follow a system that has proven long-term success and share it with others.

Step 6: Get Started

Follow your dreams, set goals, make the commitment, and write down your list. Call and invite people. Share your plan. Notice I said *share*. People like to be included in something, especially if you can personalize it for them. This is what we call the activity loop. You must act. In fact, take massive action. The more action you take toward your dream, the quicker your success will come. Step 6 determines just how long *you* decide you are going to take to reach your goal.

Step 7: Review Your Progress

You need to take a step back once in a while to see how you are really doing. Review your progress. Tweak your plan. Adjust your approach. Focus on what works. Sometimes, we get hung up on focusing on our weaknesses, thinking it will improve our success. Find your strengths, and build on those. Your success will come much faster. Use your power team to strengthen your weaknesses.

Step 8: Rotate the Pattern

This step is simple. Just keep doing everything I just talked about, over and over. Learn from your mistakes, act, and just do it. Then pay it forward.

Teach others this simple eight-step pattern!

You will learn a very important lesson, and a result is duplication. Once you learn how to duplicate, you can learn how to leverage your knowledge. Be enthusiastic, positive, and engaged. Learn how to be happy. Smile and enjoy it.

* * *

This simple pattern to success wasn't created by me. I learned this from mentors I followed throughout my business career. Dexter Yager, the world's leading network marketing expert and entrepreneur has taught and passed this pattern of success down through generations of business leaders throughout his organization worldwide. I elaborated on it as a universal success system that can be applied by any budding entrepreneur to any business opportunity. When you apply it consistently it works!

Tuesday, April 20, 2010

Soar Like an Eagle, Don't Cluck Like a Chicken

By Greg Luchak

Master Renovator, Contractor, and Entrepreneur

So why soar like an eagle? Well, better to act like an eagle than cluck like a chicken! I don't always say it, but I have often thought about it. One of my favorite speakers, Ron Ball, whom I have seen live and listened to over the years, often related stories of personal development to eagles. So, I'm basically reiterating or reinforcing, if you will, what I have learned from his teaching. In my opinion, the actions of successful people and the actions of an eagle are tremendously similar.

The eagle is the most majestic bird in the world. Eagles have the keenest eyesight. They can spot their prey from thousands of feet in the air. They can soar at tremendous speeds with their magnificent wings. They can dive downward, snapping up, clutching their prey with their talons, and are able to carry more than twice their weight. They are exceedingly independent and extremely protective of their young.

My wife and I, on our honeymoon, decided to take an Alaskan cruise. In one of the ports, we set ashore and took a wildlife tour. Our guide drove us around the shoreline, explaining the different wildlife and so on. One of the facts we were told was that the bald eagle, every summer from May to August, migrates up to Alaska. We were there at the tail end of the migration, so there were not many, but we were able to watch one as he sat atop a fifty-foot spruce tree. What he was doing was watching the salmon coming to shore to spawn. Just as we were taking our pictures, he took off, flying straight up and then swooping down onto the surface of the water, clutching what looked to be a fifty-pound salmon. It was magnificent to watch.

So where is the relevance? Take for example the behavior an eagle displays, compared to that of an entrepreneur. An entrepreneur must have vision and be able to recognize opportunity! He or she must be quick and decisive with decisions. He or she never quits. He or she never complains. Failure is not an option. Success is his or her only pursuit! He or she acts. He or she is a leader.

Now take the nature and actions of a chicken. Chickens can't fly. They can only cluck and peck and chase each other around the barnyard. You've heard the stories and comparisons of people running around like chickens with their heads cut off. Not a pretty sight, but true to life for a lot of people!

So, do you see the difference? The moral of this is simple. To be a successful entrepreneur, act like an eagle. Have great vision. Be the best at what you do. Act. Be a leader.

Soar like an eagle!

Wednesday, March 10, 2010

One Hundred Pairs of Socks Don't Count!

By Greg Luchak

Master Renovator, Contractor, and Entrepreneur

> The definition of insanity is doing the same thing
> over and over expecting different results.
> —Benjamin Franklin

Tired of being broke? Tired of the rat race? Are you desperate to have some relief from the frustration and tension? Do you want a change in your life?

The question is what motivates us? Why are you here reading this article? Why are you not watching TV? If you are like me at all, you have tried network marketing, MLM, direct sales, and real estate. You have been a seminar junky looking for that magic piece of information, looking for the next greatest ground-floor opportunity! We all think we're here for one central reason, *cash*, right? Show me the money, right? Someone said to me—and maybe this has happened to you too—"All you ever think about is money. You're so money oriented." And I tell them, "Yeah, I know. Donald Trump and I are in business to make friends. Who cares about the money, right?" I laugh when I hear people talk, when they just finished spending their last ten bucks on the lottery!

"It's not money that is the root of all evil; it's the love of money that is."

People must come to the realization that it takes money to get what you want in this world. It is an indisputable fact of life! Period!

Do you want to drive a nice car and buy it with *cash*?
Do you want to own your house, not have the bank own you?
Do you want to travel?

The question is what motivates us to reach for our goals?

Why would you want to work a business twelve hours a day, six days a week for a few short years versus working a day job for forty hours a week for the next forty years, for the rest of your life, to reach your goal?

Some people ask, "Are you insane?"

The truth is everyone is motivated by one of two things: capital gain or avoiding pain. You need to uncover your primary motivating factor. It could be any one of or all the following: extra income, financial freedom, owning your own business, more spare time, personal development, helping others, meeting new people, retirement, leaving a legacy, or whatever excites you.

The one dominating thing that you must do today to be successful in the business arena is to give value without expecting anything in return. Learn to give unselfishly. Don't think about the money. Think about the things you want to do, and plan to achieve those things.

I have a little exercise for you. Get out a pen and paper. Well first I should tell you I got the inspiration for this article from a business mentor I listen to on occasion; Reed Devries. Again just letting you know that you don't have to have an original thought of your own. You can draw inspiration from just about anywhere and from leaders you respect.

Now some of you will be able to do this in a few hours. For some of you, it will take days. Write down one hundred things you want to accomplish in your lifetime. Put them in order: financial freedom, a cash amount—and, oh yeah, one hundred pairs of socks don't count. Some of you are thinking, OK, that hokey stuff doesn't work. What doesn't work is chasing the cash. What doesn't work is being selfish with your knowledge. What doesn't work is not having a reason why.

What does work is doing something different than what you are doing right now. Remember Ben Franklin's quote! I already know that

157

most of you won't do it. Prove me wrong! For those of you who will do it, send me an e-mail, and I will show you how you can achieve your destiny with some work, of course.

Monday, May 17, 2010

Success Is a Habit

By Greg Luchak
Master Renovator, Contractor, and Entrepreneur

> Motivation is what gets you started.
> Habit is what keeps you going.
> —Jim Rohm

If you were to take the time to research any number of successful people, the one dominant trait you would find is they are creatures of predetermined habits. Often, those habits are formed by doing things repeatedly, especially activities that are uncomfortable at first, that make you stretch emotionally, physically, and psychologically as a person.

True leaders recognize that you must develop habits, create a winning attitude, and be an example to others. Develop habits that force you to be active. You must make a commitment to consistent action. Act with definite purpose, persistence, and a burning desire to reach your goal. To change your life, you need to change.

A world-renowned pioneer of motivational speaking, Earl Nightingale, once stated, "Success is the progressive realization of a worthwhile endeavor."

In other words, success is a pursuit based on persistent, consistent effort. This effort is established by creating habits that move you forward toward your goals.

Based on my own personal experience, there are five basic habits that you must establish in your life to become successful.

1. You must have a dream, a goal, a desire, and a reason why—however you label it, you must have one. If you don't know what you are reaching for, you will never reach for anything or accomplish anything.

159

2. Read! Find inspiration and knowledge from experts in all aspects of your life. Find a mentor who is active and successful in the pursuit of a common goal. Study what he or she does. If possible, get to know that person personally.

3. Take massive action. Nothing in life is obtainable without action. Your actions must be consistent and persistent.

4. Never quit! You may take years to accomplish something that you hoped would only take days or even weeks. But in the end, you will realize that the journey was just as important if not more so than the realization of your goal. Great things never come easily. The reward will always be awesome, inspiring, and invigorating.

5. You will want to repeat the process over and over, because success will become a habit!

Secret Bonus Video

www.TheWealthPrinciple.net/bonus_video.html

Success isn't about what you read.
It's about what you do!
—Gregory M. Luchak

Acknowledgments

I would like to thank the following people, who either inspired me, mentored me, or influenced me in some way to discover the knowledge that eventually led to the creation of this book.

Thank you to Napoleon Hill for all his research and inspirational books on success and how to think, along with some of his inspirational quotes, which I share in the book.

Thank you to Dexter and Birdie Yager and their sons, Jeff, Doyle, and Steve, for their consistent dedication to helping people discover their dreams and how to build a business in the process.

I would also like to thank Rich Devos and Jay Van Andel for upholding and setting the standard in business principles for anyone to follow—freedom, family, hope, and reward.

Thank you also to Andy Argyris for his personal mentorship and inspiration to chase a dream and build a business.

Thank you to Robert Kiyosaki for his simple approach to understanding how people make money and the Rich Dad seminars I attended.

Thank you to Tom Vu for his twelve-hour real estate training seminar way back in 1985 on how to negotiate the numbers and to James Smith and his M5 conference for showing me how diversified the real estate market is.

I am grateful to Tony Robbins, the king of motivational speaking, for his inspiration and books.

Thank you to Donald Trump's Trump Institute seminars I attended in Canada for showing me a few tricks on where to find capital and how to unlock it. Wow, I'll bet that will surprise a few people.

Acknowledgments

Thank you to Rita Stortini, my first real estate agent, for helping me buy my first apartment building and showing me how to get the owner to finance it.

Thank you to Ken Crosby, my first real estate lawyer, who saved my bacon on my first attempt at buying an apartment building and eventually in closing the deal on the first apartment building I did buy.

Thank you to Paul Bregman, my business lawyer in the eighties and nineties, who helped me with several real estate and business deals early in my career, and to Steve Polowin, another real estate lawyer who helped with financing a property I owned and who, without realizing it, introduced me to my first assignment deal.

Thank you to Dave Shilson for giving me Napoleon Hill's *Law of Success*, literally the bible on success from which we all draw knowledge and inspiration.

I am grateful to Aunt Jackie, who was my first paying construction client and the only family member who had faith in me.

Thank you to Frank Macmillan, another lawyer who was, first, one of my construction clients, for his help and guidance on several real estate deals.

Thank you to Coach Greg McConnell for teaching both my son Scott and me valuable lessons about coaching and leadership.

I would also like to thank Benjamin Franklin for truly explaining the definition of insanity; Google for being an endless resource to find statistics; Harry S. Dent Jr., world renowned economist, for his knowledge on demographics and the great boom ahead; and Paul Zane Pilzer, economic advisor to two US presidents and world-renowned economist, for his expertise on economic trends.

Thank you also to all those extraordinary people I have quoted throughout the book: Pope Francis, Paul Zane Pilzer, Harry Dent Jr., Dexter Yager, Napoleon Hill, John Maxwell, Albert Einstein, Tony Robbins, Kim Kiyosaki, C. S. Lewis, Holly Branson, Lori Grenier,

Robert Kiyosaki, Jim Rohm, Theodore Roosevelt, Marcia Weider, George Lucas, John F. Kennedy, Will Rogers, Donald Trump, Sir Winston Churchill, Tom Vu, Pablo Picasso, Thomas Edison, Julie Donovan, Benjamin Franklin, Richard Branson, Warren Buffet, Bill Gates, Ron Ball, Reed Devries and Earl Nightingale.

My gratitude goes to all my private clients over the years who allowed me to work with them to build their homes, additions, and renovations and fulfill a small part of their dreams and all my commercial clients and private investors who trusted me to build or renovate their investment properties over the past thirty-five years.

Thank you also to the many trusted real estate agents I worked with over the years and not in any specific order: Rita Stortini, Paul McCunn, Ajay Singhal, Thomas V. Thomas, Joe Gunn, Reina Leroux, and John and Ken Crepin. And thank you to Gerry Robert for his instructional boot camp on how to write a book successfully, which I took after I had written the original manuscript to this book, as it obviously changed everything.

And finally, I would like to thank God, to whom I give thanks for helping me find the inspiration, through perspiration, dedication, and failing forward by never, ever quitting in life. This book has been a journey that could have only been inspired by all my experiences he had to be a part of, good and bad.

Thank you all!

If you can change your perspective,

change the way you think,

you can change your life.

—Gregory M. Luchak

Index

Success Systems and Strategies

Success is a decision—your Decision!
—Gregory M. Luchak

Do *you* want more income?
Do *you* want to become an entrepreneur?

Greg Luchak

Greg Luchak often partners with individuals to create multiple sources of income. If you are serious about creating a better lifestyle and a diversified income and having more time and freedom, become an entrepreneur!

Opportunities are available to be personally coached by Greg Luchak.

www.TheWealthPrinciple.net

How It Works

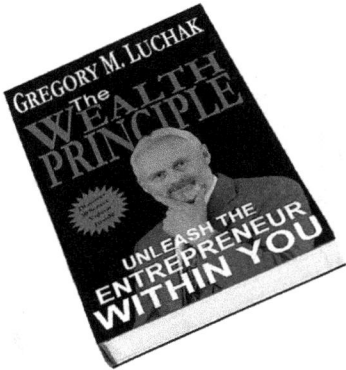

You buy books that you would then donate to a fundraiser for charity in quantities of 50, 100, 150, 200, and 250. The charity then sells the books and keeps the proceeds. As an added benefit, you get to position yourself as a sponsor of the event. You can attend and promote your business along with the author.

Become a Sponsor

Do you have a charity event you would like Greg Luchak to participate in or support?

Contact RBI Enterprises for more details on how you and Greg can become involved.

www.RealBusinessInvestors.com/contact-us

Other books, products, and services by the author

My Greatest Business and Investor Training Program
The Wealthy Renovator. (Coming in late 2018)

Videos

The Introduction
Think Like an Entrepreneur
Passion and Focus
Your Mind is Like a Parachute
Building Your Empire
Strategy! Strategy! Strategy!
Shaking the Money Tree
The Perfect Business
Becoming a Leader
Success is a Habit
The Smoked Out Condo

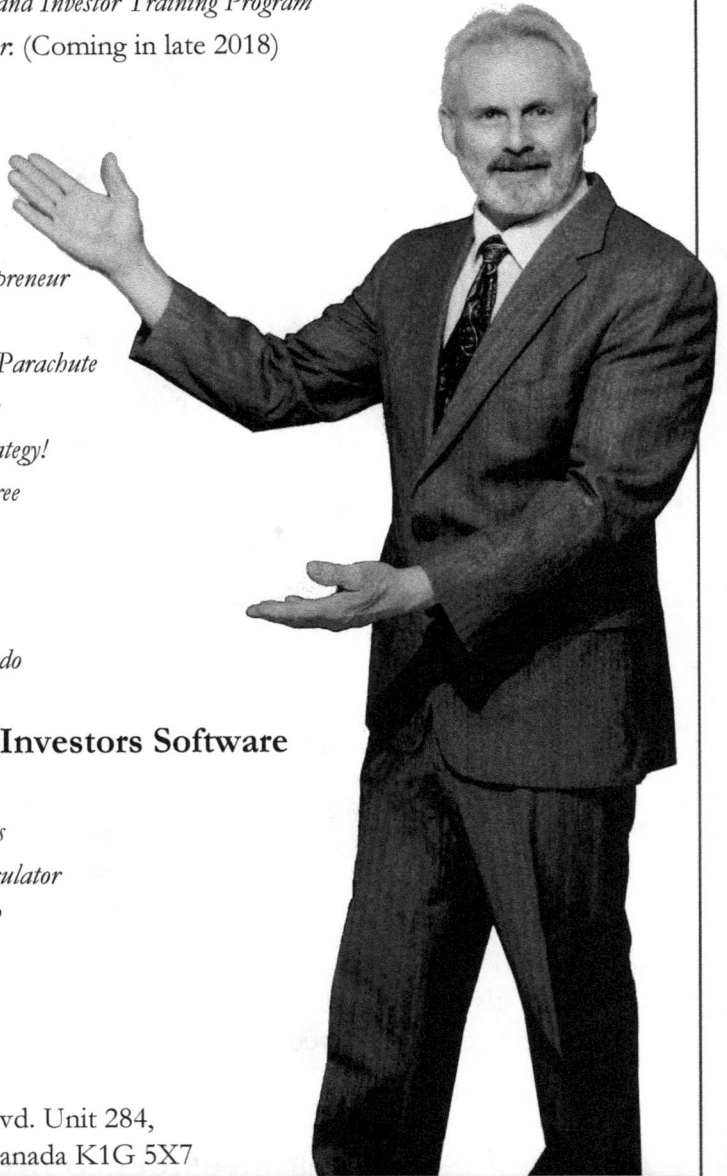

Real Business Investors Software

Real Property Investors
The Construction Calculator
The Quick Guide AP

Contact

RBI Enterprises
1769 St. Laurent Blvd. Unit 284,
Ottawa, Ontario, Canada K1G 5X7

Visit www.RealBusinessInvestors.com

About the Author

Greg Luchak

Entrepreneur, creator of My Greatest Business and Investor Training Program and Real Business Investors Software. Founder of the entrepreneurial development company RBI Enterprises and author of *The Wealth Principle*.

Greg started his entrepreneurial journey over forty years ago when he was just a teenager. He spent the past thirty-five plus years operating a construction company, investing in real estate, and flipping property. He purchased his first apartment building by the age of twenty-six.

Over that same time, Greg has helped many of his clients renovate and flip property. As a contractor, he has renovated, redeveloped, or built property ranging from residential homes and apartments to commercial fit-ups—1800s to present-day construction.

Greg's perspectives on business, money and entrepreneurship, challenge the concept—get a good education, a good job with a pension mentality. From his point of view that is fast becoming obsolete advice in today's economy. His assertion that "you must have multiple streams of income and unleash the entrepreneur within you" will prove to be the best strategy to overcome financial crisis that has impacted every generation in our current economy.

Greg's book, The Wealth Principle, will inspire budding entrepreneurs to become independent business owners. To reach for higher goals and achieve more.

To learn more about Greg's business interests scan and follow the QR codes and website links that can be found throughout the book.

RealBusinessInvestors.com

GMLuchak.com

Facebook.com/RealBusinessInvestors

PlanetOttawa.ca

YouTube.com/GregLuchak

Twitter.com/WealthPrinciple

www.ingramcontent.com/pod-product-compliance
Lightning Source LLC
Chambersburg PA
CBHW050105210326

41519CB00015BA/3829